# THE KINGDOM OF JESUS

# THE KINGDOM OF JESUS

By Roger Forster

First published in 2002 by Authentic Lifestyle

08  07  06  05  04  03  02     8  7  6  5  4  3  2

Authentic Lifestyle is an imprint of
Authentic Media, PO Box 300, Kingstown Broadway,
Carlisle, Cumbria, CA3 0QS, UK
and PO Box 1047, Waynesboro, GA 30830-2047, USA
www.paternoster-publishing.com

**British Library Cataloguing-in-Publication Data**

A catalogue record for this book is available from the British Library

ISBN 1-85078-468-X

Cover design by Diane Bainbridge
Printed in Great Britain by
Cox & Wyman Ltd., Reading

# Contents

# Foreword

One of the tragedies for the Church in the modern world has been the split between activists and the academicians, the doers and the reflectivists, the pragmatists and the intellectuals. This bifurcation at its worst leads to a) cynicism on the part of the intelligentsia who stand on the sidelines of church life finding fault and blame in every activity and human effort but contributing nothing to building up the Body of Christ, and b) frantic and frenetic energy dissipated by the 'movers' of religious life who seek to shake-off sound scholarship as if it were a hair-shirt hindering the free activity of the Holy Spirit.

There have of course been honourable exceptions to this Christian schizophrenia. Jonathan Edwards was a revivalist, a Reformed theologian and a proto psychologist. Charles Wesley was a consummate creator of demotic hymnody and a patristic scholar at Oxford. In the mid twentieth century C.S. Lewis combined a fellowship at Oxford in medieval literature with a commitment to writing popular works of Christian apologetics and tales of imagination for both children and adults.

In our own day, however, we find few men or women who can overcome the separation between head and heart, between thought and action, between practice and theory. One such person is the author of this inspirational book on the Kingdom of Jesus, Roger Forster. Perhaps best known in the evangelical world as the leader and founder of Ichthus, a radical network of Charismatic Christians in London, Roger, in partnership with his wife Faith, has been at the forefront of revivalistic enterprises literally for decades. To think of Charismatic Renewal, Spring Harvest, and the Evangelical Alliance, is to recall that Roger has been in the midst of them. Conjure-up the 'Marches for Jesus' in the 1990s and one finds that Roger helped lead them. Talk of 'Toronto' and Roger can tell you he has been in and out of it. Raise the controversial issue of 'restored apostles' and Roger can show that he has been in conversation with Restorationists over such claims for years. Imagine New Church, and Roger is the embodiment of it.

Yet amazingly this tireless activist for God, this evangelist, this builder of churches, has not forgotten the centrality to the Christian life of The Spirit's renewal of the mind. Since his Cambridge undergraduate days, Roger has never stopped learning, never remained intellectually inert, has always moved on. Consequently, it comes as quite a shock to find that the man who forsook the academy, rolled-up his sleeves, and dirtied his hands with the hard labour of mission remains as I put it in 1985 'one of the finest minds in the evangelical constituency...'. Furthermore it is a mind that breaks the mould of conventional evangelical wisdom – one that will not be fettered by dogma or rote. While many of his peers laud the foundational role of the Magisterial Reformers in the Protestant Revolution, Roger feels more at home with the radical reformation of the Anabaptists. As others nail their allegiance to Protestant Truth — denying virtually all Catholic antecedents to evangelical life – Roger empathises with Francis of Assisi, admires the Trinitarian theology of the Cappadocian Fathers of Eastern Orthodoxy, and identifies (increasingly) with much of the work of St Irenaeus of Lyon.

Conversely when Protestant evangelicals do recognise the common Christian tradition by lauding the Blessed Augustine as the defining father of Western theology, and precursor to Calvin, Roger holds him to account for most of the ecclesial and theological errors of the Western Church.

In the last year I have been privileged to work with this man of many parts and constant surprises, by teaching historical and patristic theology to the students attending the radical network course of Ichthus. I have been stunned and excited by their knowledge of biblical truth, church history, theological adventure, and the spirit of freedom in which they are encouraged to think for themselves. Roger's *modus operandi*, as a teacher and activist, is to preach, make disciples, engage in biblical exposition, evangelise, trawl the whole Christian tradition for inspiration and sub-stantiation of doctrine, try something new, then offer this unique blend of reflective activism for reappraisal and adjustment.

Much of this moving and maturing theological praxis has not been presented in scholarly tomes, or academic articles (though there are two substantial and extant co-edited works). Roger's thinking has typically been displayed in literally hundreds of audio tapes, numerous booklets, countless talks and sermons, and through personal contact. In this sense Roger is in the patristic tradition of men who wrote from within the church for the church. Recognition of his significance as an activist/theologian is evident by the fact that his work has recently been the subject of a doctoral dissertation at Leeds University and there are not many professional theologians who could say that!

This present, much needed, reflection on the Kingdom of Jesus is quintessentially Roger: the biblical exegesis reflect echoes of Tom Wright, and the recapitulation doctrine of St Irenaeus lies behind the corporate notion of Christ as embodying human kind as well as being a distinct personality in his own right. And yet the radical Charismatic and the Arminian activist is not extinguished. Roger's excitement and hope in the Kingdom shines through. He rightly sees the Kingdom as coming from outside the world, and yet recognises it as already interiorised in part by Christians within the present dispensation. But Roger does not follow Calvinist Milton in believing 'they also serve who only stand and wait': he is not 'tarrying' but remains proactive in working for the final consummation of all things when Christ will be 'all in all'.

Before Roger leads us into the mystery of the Kingdom a small caveat may help us on our journey: Roger is primarily a gospel teller in the oral tradition. He is not a systematic theologian, a representative of a definitive school of theology, a defensive personality upholding a fixed position at any cost. He is an activist who thinks – sometimes on his feet – but usually on his knees. Consequently this inspiring homily on the Kingdom is not written with the Academy in mind – you will not encounter the buttress of an academic apparatus to support it. What you will find is a message for the churches, presaged through experience, produced from an independent mind, and disseminated with love.

*Professor Andrew Walker*
*King's College, London.*

# *Introduction*

Some years go I was speaking at a college meeting when I was challenged by a Muslim sitting on the front row. He was studying Christian theology in order to destroy it and at the end of the meeting he attacked me verbally. He said, 'My lecturers cannot tell me what the Kingdom of God is and they imply Jesus didn't know what it was either'. He claimed that the Kingdom of God was such a vague concept that it was not worth preaching. In his opinion there was no coherent message – it was just an empty phrase.

The Kingdom of God, it seems, is not easily understood and has become a stumbling block for some. In the 1980s, there was an orthodox Jewish theologian called Pinchas Lapide who said he believed Jesus was raised from the dead. He maintained that the evidence for the resurrection was overwhelming and should convince anyone, but he did not believe that Jesus was the Messiah because he did not think that Jesus brought in the Kingdom.

The church is taught to pray, 'Your Kingdom come, your will be done on earth as it is in heaven' and for 2000 years Christians have prayed this prayer. But when asked, they are not at all sure of the content of their request. Do we know what we are praying for? Can we explain it to a Muslim or a Jew? Evangelical Christians are strong in their proclamation of the new birth, to be sure, but understanding it in the context of the Kingdom is vital. Unless a man or woman is born again 'he cannot see – or enter – the Kingdom' (Jn. 3:3). The Kingdom is the very *purpose* and *sphere* for which people are born again.

People have often asked me to write something about 'what on earth this Kingdom of God is'! I have been studying, reflecting on and trying to practise the Kingdom for many years. In the process, I have read much academic literature produced over the last couple of centuries, and trawled through church history to see how theologians have tried to understand the meaning of the Kingdom. In this book, I haven't gone into detail concerning my findings from these areas of scholarship, and consequently some may find it rather too simplified. My aim in writing this is not to dazzle you with historical research, but rather to try and recover the radical nature of Jesus' Kingdom message which has at times been obscured by the church culture and politics of the day.

Throughout the entire history of the church the subject of the Kingdom of God is rarely expounded. In more recent times, the higher echelons of theological thought have studied the Kingdom with renewed vigour, Joachim Jeremias, A.M. Hunter and N.T. Wright being particularly outstanding. But on the whole, neither academic nor popular theology has concentrated on this concept. We have neglected the subject, yet Jesus never stopped talking about it, never stopped preaching it. The Kingdom was the one and only message of Jesus. The very purpose of his coming was to preach the good news of the Kingdom.

Jesus' preferred title for himself was the Old Testament epithet 'Son of Man', a concept intimately linked with the

Kingdom in Daniel chapter 7. We very rarely call Jesus 'Son of Man'. We call him 'Son of God', 'Prince of Peace', 'King of Kings', 'Lord of Lords', but we do not call him 'Son of Man'. Yet this name was Jesus' favourite way of interpreting himself to the people. Jesus uses these two important verses to explain himself:

> I kept looking in the night visions and behold, with the clouds of heaven one like a **Son of Man** was coming, and He came up to the Ancient of Days and was presented before Him. And to Him was given dominion, glory and a **kingdom**, that all the peoples nations and men of every language might serve Him. His dominion is an everlasting dominion which will not pass away and His **kingdom** is one which will not be destroyed.
>
> (Dan. 7:13–14)

The church has always grappled with two fundamental questions: Who is Jesus and what was his message? These verses provide the embryonic answers: Jesus is the Son of Man and his message was the Kingdom of God. I believe that when we rediscover Jesus as the Son of Man and when we seek the everlasting Kingdom that he preached, we are going to be on track to see the end come. I want to see the end. I want the Kingdom to come. I want to see the Son of Man appearing in the clouds of divine glory and receiving to himself those that belong to him from every nation, tribe and tongue as Paul declared (1 Thes. 4:16–18). Paul didn't live to see the day – let's pray that it happens in our lifetime!

# 1

## The Centrality of the Kingdom

The centrality of the Kingdom in Jesus' teaching has been well established in recent biblical studies. It has been said that Jesus was 'obsessed' with the Kingdom. The quickest glance at the synoptic gospels reveals that there is no question that the Kingdom is what Jesus preached. In the light of the work of C.H. Dodd virtually every parable that Jesus told, whether named as a 'Kingdom parable' or not, should now be considered in the light of this his central message.

However, we see less of the Kingdom in John. The word 'Kingdom' appears more than 83 times in the synoptic gospels, yet it is used only four times in John's gospel[1]. Paul, too, only seems to refer to it some 13 times in his epistles; there are eight further mentions in Acts and seven in the rest of the epistles. These facts and figures led to an emphasis in the 19th century on the distinctions between the synoptics and John and a dichotomy emerged between the teachings of Paul and Jesus.

This emphasis, which originated in the Tübingen School in Germany, left many people confused. Was the Protestant Pauline gospel the same as the simple Good News that Jesus proclaimed? The dichotomy expressed itself as 'Jesus preached the Kingdom while Paul preached Jesus'. It is, of course, true that Paul preached Christ – the phrase 'In Christ' occurs over 160 times in his writings! In comparison, his mere 13 references to the 'Kingdom' might appear somewhat incidental. But it is significant that he preached Jesus *Christ*, the Anointed One. Jesus was anointed to be King – and where there is a King there will be a Kingdom! Paul obviously conveyed his message in Kingdom terms, especially when there was no possibility of political misunderstanding, as we see from the events in Thessalonica where Paul and Silas proclaimed Christ as King (Acts 17:7). This passage is the reversal of the cries at Jesus' execution, 'we have no king but Caesar' (Jn. 19:15).

Similarly, it would be quite wrong to say that Jesus did not preach Jesus. In the synoptic gospels he clearly put the priority of obedience to himself above any other relationship: 'If anyone comes to Me, and does not hate his own father and mother and wife and children and brothers and sisters, yes, and even his own life, he cannot be My disciple. Whoever does not carry his own cross and come after Me cannot be My disciple' (Lk. 14:26-27). He was prepared to re-interpret the law 'but *I* say unto you' (Mt. 5). He forgave sins and healed the sick, showing himself as the Lord, the healer (Ex. 15:26). He calmed the storm and walked on the sea (Job 9:8). Jesus' Kingdom message only had potency to disturb the social and political climate of his time because people were following him and looking to him to bring it about. Jesus and his message were one and the same threat to the leaders of the day (Mk. 12:12, Lk. 9:7-9).

John's gospel is equally Christocentric in its message. The seven 'I am' assertions, the three times he said 'I am that I am', and the seven 'I am...' statements with nouns, i.e. I am the bread of life, I am the Light of the World etc. are evidence alone to demonstrate that Jesus preached Jesus. 'He who has seen Me has seen the Father' (Jn.14:9) is a Christocentric claim to beat all claims![2] Just as Paul preached Jesus, Jesus preached Jesus, as well as the Kingdom.

The dichotomy between Jesus and Paul, the synoptics and John, Christ and the Kingdom is a false one. The gospels equate Jesus and the Kingdom: 'For whoever wishes to save his life will lose it; but whoever loses his life for my sake *and* the gospel's will save it' (Mk. 8:35, c.f. Mt. 16:25). 'Truly I say to you, there are some of those who are standing here who will not taste death until they see the Son of Man coming in his Kingdom' (Lk. 9:27, c.f. Mt. 16:28). Jesus said 'If I cast out demons by the Spirit of God, then the Kingdom of God has come upon you' (Mt. 12:28), thus proclaiming that his activity is Kingdom activity. God getting his will done through his Christ and by his Spirit among the people is the essence of the Kingdom. Kingdom is the King among us.

# 2

## Interpretations of the Kingdom

If we are going to make proper sense of the Kingdom of God we need first to clear the ground of some inadequate views. There have been many different understandings of the Kingdom over the centuries. Not all of them are irrelevant or totally wrong but they do not give us the whole picture, and in some cases they have misled Christian thinking.

### Augustinian (Christendom)

Since the days of Augustine many people have maintained that the Kingdom of God is to be equated with the church. When the Roman Empire collapsed, the church took over its structures and became the Holy Roman Empire. The basis of this great turn of events was Augustinian theology. Augustine is called a 'great theologian' because he influenced so many people; his thinking dominated the medieval church and was the source of what we call 'Christendom' – 'dom' for dominion or kingdom. He taught that the Kingdom of Christ was taking over the structures of power, the politics of Rome, the means of administration in society and was working through them in order to influence, control and recondition the world. The Christendom, the Kingdom of God, as understood by Augustine, was largely a political affair. The Kingdom of God grew stronger with more money, more military and more control of heretics.

Christendom grew up with its kings, princes and priests all over Western Europe. The Pope would crown the Holy Roman Emperor to show the supremacy of the church. In the Eastern side of the Empire, the Emperor ordained the patriarch of Constantinople and he was the man of power. Both of these were attempts to express the concept of the Kingdom of God as the political rule of the church through the structures of society. It is not that the church is quite one and the same with the Kingdom, according to this view, but that the church and its officials are the instrument of God's government, using the political means of secular pagan structures for implementing God's rule. Augustine was the man who laid the foundations of all church persecution when he extracted the phrase from a parable – 'compel them to come in' and misapplied it. No longer did 2 Timothy 3:12 hold true; every believer would not now 'be persecuted', rather they reigned and could persecute others. Christendom – the dominion of Christ, therefore established this kind of Kingdom of God over Europe.

But the Kingdom of God is not of this world (Jn. 18:36). It comes from outside. Quite clearly the kind of Kingdom that Jesus brings in does not have to use violence in any form. Jesus said, 'My servants do not fight'. The Christendom of the Holy Roman Empire or anything like it is not his Kingdom.

## Sovereignty

The second view, after the predominance of Augustine over the centuries, was a kind of Reformation view. At the time of the Reformation there was not much said about 'the Kingdom' but it was translated into what today is popularly called 'The Sovereignty of God', meaning, as it says in Ephesians 1:11, that God works in all things according to the counsel of his will. In this sense, the Kingdom is an inevitable, predetermined force that pervades every event because God is the chief force behind it.

However, when Paul says that God works in all things, the Greek literally says 'God in-works' – all things. This does not mean that God makes everything happen, but that God works *in* everything that happens. In other words, it is like a chess player working in the moves of his opponent in order to achieve his objective. He can use your moves to manoeuvre your knight and bishop so that your king cannot move and he gets a checkmate. He has 'in-worked' in all things. *You* put your knight and bishop there, not anyone else, but the other player made use of that and worked in it according to the counsel of his will to win the game.

If the Kingdom is God as the master chess player, manoeuvring through all the affairs and decisions of individual wills and freedoms on earth to get his will sovereignly done, it is difficult to see what the New Testament is getting at when it encourages us that 'the Kingdom of God is drawing near' (Lk. 10:11, Mt. 4:17). Jesus' view of the Kingdom is more like one of the chess pieces on the board having a radical mind of its own and becoming the effective power to implement God's will from inside the game, rather than only over-ruling it from outside. The Kingdom of God brings in a new power factor; there is a new energy on the plain of activity. The sovereignty view, though full of truth, is not adequate to explain this.

## Evolutionary

In the nineteenth century evolution was a very popular theory which was used to explain the 'origin of the species', but it also permeated many other areas of thought and study. In theology it was applied to the Kingdom of God which was conceived as moving slowly and invisibly through all the affairs of life and society from the creation of the world through the history of mankind. God is at work, secretly, bringing his purposes to fruition year by year. Eventually there will evolve from this terrific movement of God in time and space, a wonderful society, and that evolving society was called the Kingdom of God.

Parables like that of the growing seed in Mark 4:26-29 were employed to give the concept some biblical validity.

And He was saying, 'The kingdom of God is like a man who casts seed upon the soil; and he goes to bed at night and gets up by day, and the seed sprouts and grows – how, he himself does not know. The soil produces crops by itself; first the blade, then the head, then the mature grain in the head. But

when the crop permits, he immediately puts in the sickle,
because the harvest has come.'

But the point of the parable is surely not to assert that there
is a process involved in the Kingdom of God, but rather to
assure us that when you plant a seed, one day you will
inevitably reap a harvest! When you sow a Kingdom seed,
there will be a result. You do a small thing and God will do
a big thing, just how, we can't really comprehend. That was
the message of the parable, not to teach us some slowly
evolving principle!

The evolutionary view is inadequate because it involves
seeing God's working both before and after Christ as the
same thing. This would hardly fit Jesus' statement that he
was the one to introduce the Kingdom and bring it near
(Mk. 1:14-15). Something radically new had arrived.

## The Heart

The heart view is one which, although largely found in the
nineteenth century, is still very popular today. The heart
view says that the Kingdom of God is the reign of Jesus in
my heart, in my spirit, in my inner being. It appears in
many of our songs but it is not really what the Kingdom of
God is all about.

If we follow through the reasoning of this view, we are
saying that Jesus' Kingdom rule is only over his body, over
his church, over those who invite him into their heart and
let him reign there. This is not an idea that Christians

should perpetuate. It is too small. Submission and obedi-ence to God is something we should be practising anyway. It is not the wonderful thing that Jesus was talking about when he thrilled the ears of the people of his day saying, 'the Kingdom of Heaven is at hand!' When he said that people became excited. They did not say, 'that means we ought to start obeying God now' because they knew they were supposed to be doing that already. Instead they were saying, 'the Kingdom is here, God is going to do things, God is at work!'

The heart view confuses the response of believers to God, with the actual reigning of God. God is not depend-ent on our moral and ethical obedience in order to reign.

## Utopian

In the 1920s there was a very infamous Clergyman who was nicknamed the 'Red Dean of Canterbury' because he was foolishly and almost childishly impressed by Communism. He went over to Stalinist Russia, looked around (and pre-sumably did not look at the ten million peasants who were starving to death) and said, 'the Kingdom of God has come upon the earth'. His view was that the Kingdom was to bring in a perfect society, and for him at that time, Communism was it, the Utopia coined by Thomas More in his book of that title written in 1516. Sometimes this view is expressed as the 'social gospel'.

But the Kingdom of God is a gift and comes from heaven. It breaks in from the outside; it doesn't come from reconstructing our own society. 'Your kingdom *come*' implies something dramatic happening. It is a break-in; it is not something we build. We sing about it in some of our worship songs, but never in the Bible do you 'build' the Kingdom.

Jesus said, 'My kingdom is not of this world. If My kingdom were of this world, then My servants would be fighting that I would not be handed over to the Jews; but as it is, My kingdom is not of this realm' (Jn. 18:36).

## Dispensationalist

The dispensationalist view puts everything into the future. It clearly sees, and rightly so, that the Kingdom of God is eschatological, but sees no present experience or meaning for it. Consequently it relegates teaching of the Kingdom entirely to the time when Christ will come again. Some scholars have maintained that the early church fathers (before Augustine) believed in the dispensationalist view. This is not quite true. They generally believed in a future Kingdom but that does not mean that they excluded its present reality.

However for a dispensationalist the Kingdom belongs entirely in the future. So much so that I remember an elder from a denomination particularly fond of this view telling me, 'Of course, the Sermon on the Mount cannot possibly be for Christians; it is for the Kingdom when it comes. If it were for Christians now, you could ask me for my car and I would have to give it to you!' What a way to do your exegesis!

In its extreme form, dispensationalism links the Kingdom largely with Israel and the Jews. The Kingdom of God was offered to them and they refused. So, the train of the Kingdom was left on a side-track, while the gospel train rushed through the station, picked up the Gentiles and then, at the end of the age, the Hebrew Dispensational Kingdom train will be hitched up again and chug on into the Millennium. It is as though there has been a kind of hiatus hiccough between the preaching of the Kingdom which was rejected by the Jews, and its acceptance by them at the end of the age. It was to the Jews that the Kingdom was offered, in this view, not the church.

## Liberationist

In the twentieth century, Liberation theology has appeared in various guises in South America, South Africa and Korea. The basis of this view of the Kingdom is Good News for the poor. It is the poverty of the people that awakens the message of Jesus which will release them from their deprived and disadvantaged conditions and lead them into freedom. In this view the violence of revolution is an acceptable route for achieving the Kingdom using the Marxist framework for understanding conflict and ultimate rule. Jesus appears more as a Che Guevara with a gun in his hand than as the New Testament Christ of 'Father, forgive them, they know not what they do'.

While we might find many of their ideas abhorrent, there is nearly always some neglected truth to be found in every modern theology. In Liberation theology there is an emphasis on practising what you are seeking to understand. We need to participate in the truth, otherwise we will never understand it. (It is on this ground that Communists reject any Capitalistic reinterpretation of their theory.)

Jesus said much the same thing: 'If you are willing to do my will you will know'. It is those who are involved in doing his will who find they have the understanding of it. The Greeks would stand back and try to study the Bible at a distance to come up with a theology. But the Hebrews got into the Bible. They soaked in the Bible until their blood was 'bibline' and their skulls were 'inscripturated' with the view that whatever the Bible was and taught, they would become a part of it and express it. That is the only way to understand the truth of the Bible. It does not come through sitting back in an ivory tower of academia and writing books!

Despite all this good praxis in Liberation theology, there is a fundamental error in that it builds on the release of the Israelite slaves from Egypt, going through the Red Sea and entering the Promised Land. That is the Liberation motif. However, in Christian theology the story of the exodus is only a shadow of the coming liberation of Christ. It is *his* blood on the doorposts, *his* death and burial in the sea and *his* rising in resurrection power into the inheritance and promise of God. So the Liberationists' motif is the picture that is preparing the way for the reality of the Christ event and what Jesus accomplished, not a war waged against flesh and blood, but against the principalities and powers. Our liberty comes through a personal relationship with Jesus who has won our freedom on the cross, nothing else.

## World's agenda

Another view sees the condition of society as a challenge to the Christian church to 'salt and light' it and in so doing to bring in the Kingdom. This is reactive social action which follows the world's agenda. What does the world think is important? If clean drains are important, then that becomes an area for the church's operation. If the world is concerned with stemming the epidemic of AIDS then this is the job of the church. The church is here to resolve these pressing problems and it responds to the world's demands, often with little of its own agenda to present, if any at all. This is also called the 'social gospel'. I do not have any problem myself with this phrase but it misrepresents the true gospel when Christians don't preach the blood of Jesus, don't help people into a relationship with God, don't call upon God to send his Holy Spirit. Then it is simply a tinkering around with some humanistic salting and lighting to try and make life easier for people. That is the world's agenda view, and is not wrong, of course, but some people call it the Kingdom, whereas the Kingdom Jesus introduces is far more proactive, meeting all the needs of human beings – body, soul, spirit and environment.

## Structural

A recent view of the Kingdom is seen as similar to the Augustinian view, but with certain differences. The structural view, realising that lawlessness and anarchy are strong in our permissive age, seeks to introduce strong church structures of authority to compensate for the lack of order in people's lives. These structures of responsibility, sometimes called 'covering' or 'discipling', become the expression of the Kingdom of God. Living under a sort of extended pyramid authority becomes the way for salvaging the human being.

Proponents of this concept take their pattern from Deuteronomy chapter 1 and Exodus chapter 18. Moses' half-pagan father-in-law suggests a pragmatic way of dealing with the pressure of leadership over the people of Israel. Moses was to put himself on top of the pyramid with leaders below him in charge of leaders below them and so on until everyone was covered. But this is not the Kingdom of God.

It may be that the church is lacking in structure and accountability and should be much more closely knit together. We should be caring for one another, praying for one another, trying to guide, counsel and disciple, certainly. But adjusting the structures will not bring in the Kingdom. Church structure is totally pragmatic; one pattern is as good as another as long as it works – get it from your pagan father-in-law if you wish! That is not the Kingdom.

## Reconstruction or Dominion

Finally the Kingdom of God is not what is called Reconstructionist or Dominion theology. This is a comparatively new area of thought and hard to sum up because its exponents are continually changing and adapting their ideas. However this view (and it is a very noble one) calls the church to reclaim or redeem every area of society; education, business, the law, politics and so on. Proponents say that God wants to embrace every section, strata and structure of society so that they serve the purposes of the Kingdom. They believe in implementing the Old Testament law in society – which of course is largely non-Christian.

Reconstruction theology put into practice has some interesting outcomes. One real example is a fashion show where models give their testimony of what Jesus has done for them before they model the clothes. Everyone is very moved and the Spirit of God is released through the show. This is not to be dismissed out of hand. We want the Kingdom of God to invade everything. But is this actually what Jesus meant by the Kingdom?

There is also a problem with seeking to implement Old Testament law in society. It seems a difficult, if not impossible, objective, and is perhaps unacceptable even to Christians who have passed from the realm of the law to the realm of grace and mercy. The law was given to Israel, not to all the nations. Only the 'work' of the law is incumbent on the Gentile heart (Rom. 2:12-13) and Christians are no longer 'under the law' in either church life or state legislation: 'a yoke which neither our fathers nor we have been able to bear' (Acts 15:10).

The views which I have outlined describe some of the ways that people have sought to understand the Kingdom of God throughout the history of the church. In the last fifty years or so, some of these views have been more popularised because the Kingdom of God has risen to the fore of the theological agenda. So in the midst of all the grappling with the issue, why can we not find an adequate picture of the Kingdom? Surely if we are meant to receive it like children, it should not really be as difficult as all that (Mk. 10:15).

## 3

## *The Kingdom according to Jesus*

When Jesus said, 'The Kingdom of Heaven is at hand' people got excited. They must have known, roughly speaking, what he was talking about. Some of them may have got it wrong. But the Kingdom of Heaven must have been understandable in some way or other.

In broad terms we can understand how a regent exercises power in order to achieve their will in their realm. The Queen's will is exerted through her officers of state when they flash you down as you travel at a modest 100 miles an hour down the motorway. That is the Queen reigning through her body of officers. Thus, she brings her kingdom to bear on certain situations – good and bad. We do not have to persuade people that the Queen reigns over her own body, or her body of officers and gets her will done among them – that is taken for granted! The officers do the Queen's will precisely because it is their job to see that it gets done elsewhere. So too Christ reigns through his body, the church, not simply over it. The Kingdom of God is what we are talking about in the Lord's Prayer: 'Your kingdom come, your will be done on earth as it is in heaven'. God's Kingdom coming is when His will is getting done on earth. The means by which God gets his will done on earth is through his Body, the church. Through the church God releases his power and his authority into the earth. The authority is continuously coming through his Body and the power of God follows. That is releasing the Kingdom. Some people might call it releasing the Holy Spirit. That is not surprising as Paul says the Kingdom of God is 'justice, joy and peace in the Holy Spirit'. It is the Holy Spirit's release that brings these attributes of God to bear in different situations of life. Jesus said, 'If I cast out demons by the Spirit of God, then the kingdom of God has come upon you' (Mt. 12:28).

Some people don't like the phrase 'releasing the Holy Spirit' but it simply means the Kingdom coming. It is God's power and God's activity getting out to achieve his will. That is what you would expect when you think of the Queen reigning over the United Kingdom or an emperor ruling his empire. You would expect his power to be sufficient to accomplish the purposes of his Kingdom, otherwise he is no king. If the Queen's police officers were corrupt, or if they were weak and powerless and their cars could not go more than 90 miles per hour when yours tops out at 100 miles per hour, then her kingdom would collapse before long. Likewise, the Kingdom of God sometimes looks as though it is collapsing because God's chief implementer, his church, is not being the church; it is not acting like his Body. Instead it gets corrupted, running around trying to achieve its own will all the time, or else it gets inactive, flabby and weak. It is when the church is acting as the Body that it can function and release the Kingdom. There is no Kingdom without the Holy Spirit;

that is its power. And there is no Kingdom without a body to exert it. That is why the Kingdom did not appear until Jesus was a full-grown man. When he had begun his ministry and was beginning to hand his body over to us saying, 'This is my Body for you', that is when the Kingdom was really kicking into action. He gave us his body so the Kingdom could continue until he comes again. This is the Kingdom of God, and it is not too difficult to grasp. We can picture it like a dragnet that is spread right through the sea and catches fish of every kind until the time comes when the net is pulled in. When the Good News has been preached throughout the world as a witness to all nations, then the end will come. Then God sorts out the fish – the good and the bad – and separates them. But the preaching of the Good News through the world has to be done by a Body.

Now when Jesus proclaimed 'the Kingdom of Heaven is at hand', there were at least four expectations that arose in the minds of those that heard him preach (see also J. Jeremias *Introduction to the New Testament*):

1) The presence of God by his Holy **Spirit**.
2) The overcoming and the defeat of **Satan**, his kingdom and evil.
3) **Salvation** offered to all – the full-blooded rehabilitation and wholeness of humanity.
4) A New **Society** that was being brought into being.

In the following chapter we shall take a look at each of these aspects of Jesus' teaching on the Kingdom of God.

## Here comes the King!

When the Jews heard the message, 'Repent, the Kingdom of God is at hand' they were looking for God's presence coming among his people. They expected God to make himself present and available to them and to be poured out without measure. They would call to mind the Old Testament prophets who were looking forward to a great day in the future: the day of the Lord – 'I will pour out My Spirit on your offspring and My blessing on your descendants' (Is. 44:3), 'I will pour out my Spirit on all mankind...' (Joel 2:28).

In fulfilment of these prophecies, the Holy Spirit anointed Jesus as King at his baptism, and began flowing out from him, the fountain-head, to be made available without measure to all people. 'I baptize you with water' (i.e immerse, drench, saturate) said John, 'He (Jesus) will baptize you with the Holy Spirit and fire' (Lk. 3:16). God is now completely and unreservedly accessible by his Spirit, available without limitation. Pentecost was the evidence of this outpouring, and the fire was accompanied by a wind which was understood as God's breath or Spirit in the Old Testament:

> For He will come like a rushing stream
> Which the wind* of the Lord drives.
>
> (Is. 59:19)
>
> (*Hebrew 'wind' can mean either 'breath' or 'spirit')

Paul describes the Kingdom of God as 'righteousness, peace and joy in the Holy Spirit' (Rom. 14:17). This sounds a bit like the exuberance of Pentecost! The evangelism which followed was about making this same Holy Spirit available to the rest of mankind: 'God...also made us adequate as servants of a new covenant, not of the letter, but of the Spirit; for the letter kills, but the Spirit gives life' (2 Cor. 3:6).

The Kingdom of God coming meant that the King had arrived. The people who heard Jesus' proclamation knew to expect the tangible presence of God by his Spirit.

## War declared

Jesus announcing the imminence of the Kingdom of God in his first recorded sermon was a declaration of war on Satan. People hearing it expected that the devil would be defeated. They believed that the Kingdom of God would wage war on the kingdom of darkness and that Satan would be cast out.

Satan's defeat is clearly depicted in the wilderness temptation conflict (Mt. 4:1-11), where Jesus emerges as victor. However, it is at the Cross that the evil forces of the universe are finally confronted and put into total disarray: 'When He had disarmed the rulers and authorities, He made a public display of them, having triumphed over them through Him (Jesus)' (Col. 2:15). Now Satan, the strong man of Matthew 12:24-29, can be bound, and God's liberating forgiveness released through his servants: 'If you forgive (release) the sins of any, their sins have been forgiven (released) them; if you retain the sins of any, they have been retained' (Jn. 20:21-23). This victory was prophesied in the beautiful Isaianic passage in which the enemy's weapons, sickness, sin and death are wrested from his grasp and a stronger champion divides the spoil of his resurrection triumph with his followers (Is. 52:13–53:12, c.f. Lk. 11:22). Jesus' words in Mark 10:45 contain at least four allusions to the 'servant' passages of Isaiah 52 and 53: 'For the Son of Man came not to be served but to serve' (Is. 52:13), '...and to give his life as a ransom' (Isa. 53:10) '...for' (Is. 53:4–6) '...many' (Is. 53:11–12).

As God's servant Moses was used to ransom Israel from Egypt, so Jesus would ransom his people from mankind's greater enemy. 'Now judgment is upon this world; now the ruler of this world will be cast out. And I, if I am lifted up from the earth, will draw all men to Myself' (Jn.12:31) declared the new King, Jesus. Evangelism, preaching the good news of the Kingdom, is demonstrating that Satan is defeated: 'The seventy returned with joy, saying, "Lord, even the demons are subject to us in Your name." ' (Lk. 10:17–20).

## The Lord saves

The Kingdom of God is at hand! Salvation has dawned! The saving powers of the coming age have arrived! The people understood it because the prophet Isaiah had foretold it:

> Your dead will live;
> Their corpses will rise

> (Is. 26:19)

And on that day the deaf shall hear words of a book,
And out of their gloom and darkness the eyes of the blind shall
see.

(Is. 29:18)

Then the eyes of the blind will be opened,
And the ears of the deaf will be unstopped.

(Is. 35:5)

The Spirit of the Lord God is upon me,
Because the Lord has anointed me
To bring good news to the afflicted;
He has sent me to bind up the brokenhearted,
To proclaim liberty to captives,
And freedom to prisoners;

(Is. 61:1)

This salvation is evident enough in Jesus ministry for John
the Baptist to be satisfied that he was the expected Messiah
coming to bring in the Kingdom: 'The blind receive sight,
the lame walk, those who have leprosy are cured, the deaf
hear, the dead are raised and good news is preached to the
poor' (Mt. 11:5, c.f. Lk. 7:22). In this way Jesus announces
the fulfilment of God's salvation purposes for men.

'Blessed is the man who does not fall away on account of
me' (Mt. 22:11). Why should the disciples be tempted to fall
away? No doubt because the peaceful blessings that Jesus
spoke of seemed to exclude the use of violence against the
Jews' Roman oppressor. The sort of salvation that Jesus had
come to bring was not the sort won by an aggressive

Messiah. Rather the hour had come when '...the (spiritually) dead shall be raised' and when 'true worshippers will worship in Spirit and truth' (Jn. 5:25, 4:24). The new covenant where sins are no more remembered by God had arrived at last (Jer. 31:33-34). Salvation had really come.

Two symbolic actions, based on Zechariah's prophecy, performed at the beginning and end of his ministry declared, along with Jesus' Kingdom message, how completely the New Age had intervened. First, Jesus cleansed the temple (Jn. 2:14-17, Mk. 11:15-17) 'so that there should be no longer a merchant in the house of the Lord Almighty' as Zechariah declared in Zechariah 14:21. This demonstrated that the age of true worship had come. Secondly, he rode into Jerusalem as Zechariah had predicted, 'See your King comes to you, gentle and riding on a donkey' (Zech. 9:9, Mt. 21:5, Jn. 12:15). The prophet goes on to describe the universal peace God's kingdom would bring by removing the instruments of war and proclaiming peace to the nations:

I will cut off the chariot from Ephraim
And the horse from Jerusalem;
And the bow of war will be cut off.
And He will speak peace to the nations;

(Zech. 9:10)

Evangelism is preaching the kingdom of grace to eternal life (Rom. 5:21) and evoking faith in men and women to enter it and be saved: 'Much more then, having now been justified by his blood, we shall be saved from the wrath of God through him' (Rom. 5:9).

# A new people

Thus three of the expectations of the Kingdom held by the Jews in Jesus day were fulfilled in him: when Jesus preached the Kingdom he also demonstrated the presence of God, the defeat of the kingdom of darkness and the offer of salvation. But fourthly, they also expected a new people to come into being – the formation of a new society. They saw it in the Old Testament; some thought of it as exclusively Jewish and others thought it would include the Gentiles. But this is not quite the Kingdom. There would certainly be a new Kingdom people who would act as the vehicle for the operation of the Kingdom of God, but the Kingdom of God and the people of the Kingdom need to be distinguished; they are not the same thing. I am sorry to be pedantic but you will find all these things confused in popular ideas of the Kingdom. You don't say that the Kingdom of England is all the people who live in it; it would exist even if nobody lived there! The Kingdom of God is not the people; it is the authority of God achieving God's will on earth as it is in heaven by the release of power through his people.

This distinction between the Kingdom and its people is made in Matthew 21:43, together with a further distinction between the Kingdom and its fruit: 'The Kingdom of God (the Kingdom) will be taken away from you and given to a nation (the people of the Kingdom) producing the fruit (the fruit of the Kingdom) of it'. The fruit of the Kingdom is the effects of God getting his will done through his Kingdom people.

In Jesus' Kingdom a new society is born. The poor have Good News preached to them. Jesus is using verses which Isaiah has coined on the basis of Leviticus 25, the jubilee programme of Israel, known as the year of restoration (Lk. 4:18,19). This kind of society came into being spontaneously after Pentecost (Acts 2:42-47; 4:32-37) as the disciples practised jubilee living.

However, Jesus' preaching of good news to the poor went beyond just the materially disadvantaged. He included the spiritual bankruptcy of tax collectors and prostitutes (Mk. 2:16; Mt. 21:32; Lk. 7:37-39) provoking the derisive title 'friend of sinners' from his enemies (Mt. 11:9). This beautifully sums up Jesus' own interpretation of good news to the poor. These could come near to God, for God had drawn near to them. They could receive his rest, forgiveness and life by faith for no price. This same condition made it hard for the financially and morally rich ruler to inherit eternal life (Mt. 19:13-26).

We need empty hands to receive Christ's resources, as dependants with no independent means to fall back on! We come as new-born children into our Father's kingdom. The 'poor' include the sick, the oppressed, the broken hearted (Is. 61:1-3), the prodigal son and the dying thief. All these are welcomed into the Kingdom of God to find release, healing and forgiveness in the new community of God's people. Evangelism is introducing people into the richness of Christ's new society:

> But you have come to Mount Zion and to the city of the living God, the heavenly Jerusalem, and to myriads of angels, to

the general assembly and church of the firstborn who are enrolled in heaven, and to God, the Judge of all, and to the spirits of the righteous made perfect, and to Jesus, the mediator of a new covenant, and to the sprinkled blood, which speaks better than the blood of Abel (Heb. 12:22-24).

The advent of Jesus means the Father's kingdom has intervened into the affairs of men. This does not mean that God has never reigned before. He has an eternal kingdom and has been ruling in the kingdoms of mankind from the very beginning of history: 'For his dominion is an everlasting dominion, and his kingdom endures from generation to generation' (Dan. 4:32-34) leading men to *repentance*.

But now God's kingdom is present and able to be received as it rescues and delivers with signs and wonders: 'And his kingdom is one which will not be destroyed, And his dominion will be forever. He delivers and rescues and performs signs and wonders in heaven and on earth' (Dan. 6:26,27). This kingdom is received by *faith*.

But God's kingdom is also future: 'The God of heaven will set up a kingdom which will never be destroyed, and that kingdom will not be left for another people; it will crush and put an end to all these kingdoms, but it will itself endure forever' (Dan. 2:44). All opposition will be removed and sorrow and tears will disappear. His servants will reign with him in the New Jerusalem golden society for ever and our lives will be orientated in *hope*.

Therefore in the light of God's reign, mankind is called to *repentance*, *faith* and *hope* in order to participate fully in God's Good News of the Kingdom. It is received by grace, 'Fear not, little flock, it is my Father's good pleasure to give you the kingdom' (Lk. 12:32). The love, justice and forgiveness of God, seen in the society of his people, reveal the heart and character of the Father to a broken-down world. This new society acts as salt in the old society, hindering corruption and fertilizing spiritual growth (Mt. 5:13). It lights up the world to relieve its darkness and check its evil ways. It is expressed in power through his people by works of healing: '…and heal those in the cities who are sick, and say to them, "The kingdom of God has come near to you"' (Lk. 10:9, 17-22) and forgiveness: 'If you forgive the sins of any, their sins have been forgiven them' (Jn. 20:21-23). The mission of Jesus continues through his people, bringing his Kingdom into the lives of men and women.

The Kingdom extends to all nations: 'This gospel of the kingdom will be preached to the whole world', and it has a consummation: '…and then the end will come' (Mt. 24:14). At the final consummation of all things, Jesus will return to root out all that offends at his reign and will divide the wise and foolish, good and lazy, faithful and wicked, sheep and goats, for his eternal reign of righteousness and love. The King will reply, 'I tell you the truth, whatever you did for the least of these brothers of mine you did for me…take your inheritance, the kingdom prepared for you since the creation of the world…'(Mt. 25: 21, 26, 40, 34).

But first, this gospel of the Kingdom must be preached in all the world! This is a dangerous assertion because a Kingdom is a political concept. Jesus was crucified as a political offender who was 'no friend of Caesar'. So, what kind of politics were around in Jesus' time? Howard Yoder and others have identified four. The next chapter takes a look at these.

## 4

# *The Politics of the Kingdom*

When one speaks of the Kingdom the very term immediately evokes political understanding and ideas. If Jesus is the King and there is a Kingdom which is breaking in and is at hand, it must be in opposition to other kingdoms. The ultimate message of the gospel is that the kingdoms of the world shall become the Kingdom of our God and his Christ. So, there is a declaration, in a sense, of one political structure versus all the others that exist.

The political overtones of 'the Kingdom' therefore cannot be avoided, and they are clearly in evidence when Paul preached the Kingdom of God. It may be for this reason that only eight times in the Acts and a few times in the epistles we find Paul using the term 'the Kingdom of God'. He uses the word 'king' prolifically – a Messiah, Christ – but this is almost a euphemistic way to avoid the political confrontation all the time because quite evidently in Thessalonica preaching Jesus as King was as confrontational as Jesus before Pilate when the Passover crowd cried, 'we have no other King but Caesar'. Consequently the whole Roman Empire would be opposed to the Kingdom proclamation of Jesus. Paul might well have made some accommodation to this, without losing the essence of what the Kingdom of God is about.

As 'kingdom' is a political term, equally 'Good News' (euangelion) is also political. It was used at the birth of the emperor's son and heir, and it was used at the accession of a new emperor. It was bread and games for all the people; a holiday was declared and free handouts distributed. It was called an evangel, good news. When this term was used, people would respond and know, to some degree, what it was about.

Jesus himself was crucified by the Romans between two criminals. He was a political offender in terms of the society that put him to death. The criminals he died alongside were almost certainly insurrectionists; this was certainly true of Barabbas who was seeking to bring down the Roman government. It is not surprising, therefore, that Jesus was seen to be a political threat. When we talk about the difficulties we have today in preaching the gospel to the world, into a post-Christian world or a Muslim world, don't let us forget the hostility that would have been evoked in preaching that a criminal executed by the Roman government, in actual fact was the Lord of all. This was appallingly offensive and not conducive to being culturally acceptable, but nonetheless they proclaimed it. We have to go out with the truth and trust that the Spirit of God brings it home to human hearts. That was the way the gospel spread through the world in the first century.

At the time of Jesus there were four different parties holding different political stances in Israel. By taking a look at them we can understand more clearly the context into which Jesus' Kingdom message came (c.f. Yoder, *The Politics of Jesus*).

## Zealots

The first group were the Zealots who were to be found among Jesus' disciples, one in particular is named as Simon the Zealot. They were clearly an organised group of 'liberation theology' activists. They wanted to overthrow the government and believed that Israel should be a free nation for the sake of Jahweh. Israel had not been free for centuries, from the time of the exile in the days of Nebuchadnezzer (606 BC through to 586 BC). From the exile onwards the smaller, southern kingdom of Judaea had been politically dominated by the empires of the world because even when the people were permitted to come back and rebuild their Temple it was all under the sovereignty of the Persian Empire. Then the Greeks took over and, dividing into four parts, governed Israel until the Maccabees threw them off in the second century BC. But this did not last very long because the Romans were soon on the doorstep and ready to break in. They finally took over Jerusalem and the new age of the Roman Empire had begun with Pompey's triumph in 61 BC. Only a few years of hard won independence were enjoyed by the Jews during nearly 550 years of occupation.

The Zealots wanted back the days of the Maccabees' liberation and political independence and they were prepared to use violence to achieve their aim. There are many parallels with similar situations today and the response of Liberation theology. There are always those who contend for the underdog, the one who has been oppressed, claiming their day of freedom and independence. Unfortunately they often forget that the oppressed quickly becomes the oppressor and the cycle is perpetuated. Jesus was not going to get into that kind of battle and instead he took 'the way of peace you did not know' to Jerusalem. Having a Zealot like Simon in his team mixed up with ex-quislings like the tax collector Matthew was an amazing accomplishment. The Lord's personality, power and spiritual authority must have been stupendous to be able to weld together such a diverse bunch of people. We expect the same Holy Spirit to do that with us today.

## Pharisees

The Pharisees had their roots back in the same period of the Maccabees. Israel, which had been occupied since the exile, had been placed under Antiochus Epiphanes who was a tyrant of no small order. The hostility and hatred awakened in Israel would cause them to fight to the very end; the great strength of the Maccabean movement overthrew the rule of the crumbling Greek Empire, and they finally overcame. Israel, then, for a short period, was free. However, sadly, as so often happens, the newly-established leaders became increasingly oppressive to their people. They took honours to themselves, such as the high priesthood to which they were never entitled, and they alienated themselves from the popular understanding of holiness.

In reaction to this worldly government, the Hasidim were a party fanatical in their devotion to holiness. Under the Greeks they struggled for religious liberty but later gradually withdrew from any political involvement. The Pharisees emerged as a party during the second century BC and continued the tradition of the Hasidim. They, also, avoided the whole governing structure, but they still enjoyed the benefits the structures provided for them.

The same can happen with Christians today. There are Christians who take the Zealot stance. In parts of South America, Africa or Asia, Liberation theology thrives because Christians are concerned to bring Good News to the poor by relieving them of the structures which make them poor. Some, in that situation, feel it is quite accept-able to say, 'we want to be Zealots; we want a theology which allows us to fight!' But the Pharisees who stand back from that and say, 'Politics are dirty; that's not the way of Jesus' will often still happily accrue the benefits from the Zealots' activism, if they do bring liberation to the country. If the Zealots do not win and the alternative party rules the day, then the Pharisees can obtain benefits from that party instead. This kind of abstinence falls short of making a person of real integrity. Should I really reap the benefits of other people's labour when I refuse to return anything for them? Jesus did not seek to actively follow the agenda of the politics of his day. Neither was he apolitical. His very use of the word Kingdom, and all the content of it that he demonstrated, preached an alternative politic – the politics of God instead of a man-made system. Some Christians today opt out of politics altogether. This may be the right thing to do, but too often the motive is wrong. They take this stance because they believe there is a higher calling upon their lives which exempts them from concerning themselves with political issues. This was precisely the case with the Pharisees.

## Sadducees

The Sadducees were another party named in the New Testament. They were the capitalistic rich, the ruling party of Jesus' day. The high priest, Caiaphas, who was a Sadducee (most of the priestly party were Sadducees) was the richest man of those times. His business in the Temple courts was only a side-line to his money-making all over the nation. There was one time when at least one third of Israel's wealth lay in the Temple coffers – and the Sadducees administered that money, so they were very powerful people. There was one occasion during this period when the Romans even borrowed money from the Temple. Caiaphas, and Annas his father-in-law, knew how to handle such situations; they negotiated and gained benefits for their people, whilst at the same time bolstering their own interests.

All other subjugated nations had to fight for the Romans but the Sadducees negotiated an exemption from military service for the Jews. Every other nation in the Roman Empire was obliged to worship the Emperor, but the Jews were excepted. It was for this reason that Christians were, for a while, tolerated by the Roman Empire; they were regarded as a licit religion under the Jewish advantages which had been accrued for them. As soon as Christianity was seen to be a heretical sect of Judaism dominated by Gentiles, the persecution began in earnest.

The Jewish people in the first century AD received and supported the Sadducees because they were rich and powerful men who could stand up to the Romans and secure benefits for them. At the heart of this state of affairs is the reasoning which lies behind all straight-forward capitalist systems; it is necessary to have some rich people in the system to benefit the whole population – if everyone is poor no-one is benefited.

As well as Zealots and Pharisees, there are also Sadducees in the church today who say, 'We need to get into the structures of politics and wield them to gain advantages for our people and for the church!' But when did Jesus ever tell us to make sure of our own well-being and demand our rights as the church? He *did* say that we were around to wash feet and take Good News to the poor. Looking after our own self-interest is something different. Unfortunately, if you dig down far enough, you find that some of those who pray fervently for their nation are generally thinking of achieving a nicer society for Christians! It might be desirable to have benefits for the church, but it is far better to serve those outside of it. We need to watch our motives as we pray for our country, that we do not simply seek an asier life from the answers. Should we not rather be concerned to bless every other human being on the planet?

## Essenes

Unlike the three preceding parties, the Essenes are not named in Scripture. They were part of a movement among the people some of whom withdrew from the realm of everyday life and politics to form their own communities. The Dead Sea Scroll sect at Qumran was clearly an Essene expression, and a great deal has been discovered about the beliefs and practices of these people. They produced a very interesting kind of community life and it would seem that in many ways Jesus' teaching was closer to the Essenes than to the other three parties. There are obvious parallels to be drawn, too, with the community life initiated by the power of the Holy Spirit in the Acts of the Apostles.

The language of John's gospel echoes the language of the Dead Sea Scrolls and in it Jesus is seen to be using a particular style to communicate into that area of thought. The high ideals of the Essenes approximate to Jesus' ideals perhaps more than any of the other parties. The Essenes were passivists but they believed that they would engage in violence at the last great battle when the Messiah would lead them against the forces of evil, often pictured as a war between darkness and light (Jn. 1:5).

The Essenes, however, are not mentioned by name in the New Testament. The link is, perhaps, through John the Baptist. The gospel writers describe John as 'one who was like a voice crying in the wilderness'. John was almost certainly an orphan because his parents were so old when he was born. It is known that a great feature of the Essenes was that they took in abandoned children and brought them up within their own society. Another pointer is that they practised ritual washings – baptisms – which was almost unknown among the Jews. It was generally held that only a proselyte (that is a Gentile becoming a Jew) needed to be baptised. But John the Baptist came preaching baptism for repentance for Jews. We cannot be sure that John was an Essene but it is possible.

The Essenes lived as separatists from the structural system of Israel. One of the reasons for them establishing a community on the Dead Sea was that they repudiated the high priests and the priestly caste in Jerusalem. They considered the priesthood to be corrupt and illegitimate, as the priests were not descendents of Aaron. They were right on both counts. The Essene answer to the corrupt system of the Temple was total separation from Jewish religion and politics. Instead they sought to create a beautiful society, a utopia, living together in obedience to God. This is the kind of aspiration that motivated Christians in the early chapters of the Acts. Again and again in human society there has been the desire for shared living and common life. Some have expressed it in monasteries, others in the brethren of common life from which Thomas à Kempis, Erasmus and others have emerged. The Anabaptists, the Hutterites, the Mennonites, and many substrata escaped across to the Americas to try and set up their perfect communities, some becoming particularly heretical like the Mormons, some becoming totally atheistic and establishing their commune without God's help. None of these attempts seemed to be overly successful but they were all good attempts to bring in a more satisfying life by living and sharing together.

Communism has its roots in communes which are historically rooted in Christian aspirations for a greater and richer style of living and sharing together. The Qumran society falls into that particular political stream, rejecting everything concerned with the Temple in Jerusalem. For that reason the only sacrifice they practised was that of the red heifer because it was the one sacrifice that could be performed outside of Jerusalem. It is interesting to note that this is referred to in the book of Hebrews (9:13) and the question arises as to whether the writer of this book was referring to Christians who had come out of the Qumran type of society. The inference is that they were tending to go back to the community for protection since Christians and Jews were separating and Christianity was coming under persecution. This, of course, is another subject but it shows that there are possible points of contact in the book of Hebrews and in John the Baptist with the Essenes and the Qumran society.

The Essene political response, then, was to abandon the structures of society and set out their own perfect Kingdom of Heaven. They founded an alternative subculture where they intended to live their lives for God in peace, godliness and holiness, and let the world around corrupt. The difference with Jesus was that he wanted to build the new Jerusalem within the context of the old society. He wanted to enter into the city rather than abandon it for the wilderness. Jesus takes us out into all the world, in all its spheres and connotations, in order to express God's politics by acting as salt to resist the world's corruption. In Jesus we are given the power of the Kingdom of God to introduce into every strata of society – we are not meant to take it away and use it exclusively for ourselves.

There isn't a political party that quite fulfils these kinds of Kingdom conditions, and I would suggest that the church has to rethink its political stance and involvement at all levels. How it functions will probably vary according to the situation. But there is no straightforward, simplistic answer to what a Christian's political stance or allegiances should be. The politics of Jesus are very clear – he *is* them! Politics are essential for human life and community relations. The art of government in itself is not bad and need not be coercive, but it should preserve a framework for true freedom to exist amongst men and women. Jesus, however, seems to have his own unique way of doing politics. 'The Kings of the Gentiles lord it over them, and those who have authority over them are called "Benefactors" But not so with you. But let him who is the greatest among you become as the youngest, and the leader as the servant' (Lk. 22:25-26). The Jesus criteria for government are no status and servanthood. The world teaches leaders to work hard to become something special so that they can influence and dominate people. The mission the church has in the world, however, is symbolised by the basin and the towel, by getting down upon our hands and knees and washing people's feet, just as Jesus did in John 13. This requires vulnerability, involvement, participation, gentleness and care. These are not the qualities to be found in most politicians, party leaders or rulers, neither do they stand out as the main values sought after in democratic electorates.

The world has yet to see a body – or even a party – of people who will govern the Jesus way, with the Jesus criteria, the basin and the towel. A revolution based upon such principles could be the answer to the world's tired and worn-out politics.

# 5

# *The Kingdom and Holy War*

In the days of Jesus the Jews to whom he ministered would have had many preconceptions of the Kingdom of God. Their understanding would have been framed, in part by ideas of 'holy war' from the Old Testament. There are many stories of how God stepped in in the days of Moses, Joshua, Samuel and so on, to overthrow the enemy. It was God who was doing the fighting. Although they often did not have to do very much, the Israelites were brought in on the war and sometimes added their bit of fighting. Sometimes God delegated his authority – as in the slaughter of the Canaanites or the administering of capital punishment. There is nothing wrong in God giving life and nothing wrong in his taking it; it belongs to him. Morality, right and wrong, only comes into it when *we* begin to exercise authority to take life. That may be immoral, depending on whether or not the authority has been delegated from the One who has the right to it. The taking of life is something which is God's alone and, of course, he does it with us all in the end when he takes our life from us in death. God may have delegated his authority for that particular, one-off experience of the slaughter of the Canaanites and Amalekites on route to the Promised Land, but Jesus made it clear that he was not going to use the sword, and neither were we.

In passing, it seems to me that until Jesus came there were certain things that God had to do which were expedient rather than absolute or ideal. The expediency of the slaughter of the Canaanites was that God delegated to Israel the removal of that race after 400 years of patiently waiting for them to change their ways, for they were a corrupt people. In Genesis it says that God would not destroy them by Abraham because the people still had not come to the fullness of the sin and, presumably, that meant that until they did, he would not act. But when he did act, he brought in the children of Israel as a kind of surgical instrument (this is a speculative understanding of events in the Scripture). The surgical knife was to cut out the cancer from the body of the human race that left unchecked, would have corrupted the whole.

As we read the Old Testament we need to understand that the abominations that went on were absolutely abysmal. There was sexual perversion and sacrifice of children. God's knife cuts out the cancer in order that the whole human race might be recovered. Israel's part is to take the place of the diseased section. That is the way I understand the delegated function of the use of the sword by Israel from God. Then when Jesus comes, the cure has arrived – the salt of society, the light of the world. Now this medicine can be applied to the human race instead of surgery and hence it says he does not use a sword: 'If my Kingdom were of this world then…fight!' (Jn. 18:36, Mk. 22:49-53, Mt. 26:52).

In other Old Testament instances, holy war was executed only in defence when other armies were coming in to try and destroy Israel, and, generally speaking that defence was God's battle rather than theirs. They had to turn up on occasions, sometimes without any armaments, like in the days of Jehoshaphat (2 Chr. 20) when they all stood and worshipped with their wives and little ones (v13). As they worshipped, over in Edom the Moabites and Ammonites all began to fight one another and so the danger was averted. Again, at the time of Deborah (Judg. 4-5) when she pushed Barak into the front line against the Canaanites, a great storm completely destroyed the enemy's superior weaponry, namely the advanced chariots they had developed which the Israelites did not have. Again and again in the Old Testament it says, 'some trust in horses, some trust in chariots, but we will trust in the name of the Lord'. The Lord refused to let Israel have horses and chariots and the usual weapons of war that the surrounding nations would use to conquer. It was only when Solomon inherited his father David's throne that he brought in such martial equipment from Egypt. Until then, the Israelites were expected to trust in God alone; God did the fighting – 'the battle is the Lord's'.

Looking back at the Law and the Prophets, Jews in the days of Jesus would have inherited a warfare worldview of God's purposes, before Jesus came preaching the Kingdom of God. God would at times give them the right to fight, but basically he would come through and do the fighting himself. It is not surprising that for the average person in Israel, the idea of war was not incompatible with the ways of God. War was an accepted and expected means of liberation because of the Old Testament stance and the history of Israel. When people looked to Jesus as the Messiah, the Christ, they expected the Kingdom of God to come with the use of the sword. That is why Jesus was so very careful in how he presented himself. If he had gone around saying, 'I am the Messiah' it would have just fed the popular misconception that the perfect and preferred way of God is surgery, not medicine. They would have expected Jesus to take up the sword and lead them into battle against the Romans so that Israel could be independent again. God could have a people for himself again, and they would have plenty of room to be kings and rulers, on behalf of Jahweh, of course! They would reign, albeit for the Lord's sake, and thus the Kingdom of God would be established.

Therefore, Jesus did not often openly declare himself the Messiah lest he be misunderstood. So much so, that some have imposed upon every Scripture, a concept called the 'Messianic Secret'. The theory is that Jesus deliberately concealed his Messiahship, and I think there is a certain amount of truth in it. There are probably other reasons why he kept it quiet. It is rather remarkable that the only person with whom he freely shared that he was the Christ, without it being elicited from him, was the woman of Samaria. When she said, 'I know when the Messiah comes, He will reveal all things', he volunteered, 'I am He that speaks to you'. He did not do that to anybody else, as far as is recorded in the Scripture.

When Peter said 'You are the Christ, the Son of the Living God', Jesus said, 'Flesh and blood has not revealed it to you but my Father'. The Father revealed it in Peter's heart and he spoke it out. Jesus did not say it to Peter, although he did not deny it. Again, when Jesus is put on oath before the high priest: 'Tell us whether you be the Christ, the Son of the Living God,' he says, 'I am as you say and you will see the Son of Man coming in power'. He introduces the concept of the Son of Man, rather than use the more inflammatory 'Messiah'.

So Jesus was deliberately avoiding a violent politics-type approach which would have played to the misconceptions of the Jews. However the misconceptions were understandable on the basis of their history. The whole of Jesus' ministry is a re-interpetation and re-reading of the purposes of God in choosing Israel, in stark contradiction to the dominant view.

Jesus is introducing a higher understanding of what the Kingdom of God is about, but it must be seen in the context of how the Jews had understood the Kingdom in the Old Testament days. They knew they had experienced some kind of Kingdom; they knew they had lost it; they knew it was to come again. They knew it was to break-in with power, so when Jesus declared 'the Kingdom of God is at hand' they expected, of course, that this was a wholesale battle. Even the Qumran society – a community of non-combatants and pacifists – allowed that in the last great battle when the Messiah came, they would actually fight. It is for this reason that so much fighting took place in Israel, not only in Jerusalem but also in Masada, with Jewish people thinking, believing or hoping that this was the last great battle. There were no total pacifists in the Jewish scene of Jesus' day. There were only partial pacifists who believed that they would one day fight in the last great battle.

Jesus totally repudiates the use of violence for the extension of his Kingdom. 'If my Kingdom were of this world,
My servants would fight, but My Kingdom is not of this
world, therefore they do not fight'. Fighting is excluded by
Jesus as far as advancing the Kingdom of God is concerned.
Never are we to be tempted to think that the use of the
sword, however much it was used in the Old Testament, can
advance the Kingdom of God. The Kingdom of God must
be established, not on other people's blood, but on our own
blood and on the blood of Jesus. That means it will last forever. When you try to build a kingdom by violence, you
breed more violence which breeds more violence. In the
Old Testament story of David and Saul, David knew that he
couldn't kill Saul in order to take over the kingdom, because
if he did so, somebody would kill David and somebody
would kill David's killer and so on. That is the story of the
history of the human race; you reap what you sow. A kingdom built on violence cannot last. Thank God that his
Kingdom rules through the cross – 'King' was written over
him as he died. The Kingdom was founded on Jesus' own
blood, not on his enemies.

So, how are we to reinterpret the bloody history of Israel
in Jesus' terms of peace? In the Old Testament there are
three things that we can note about Holy War:

1) God would do the fighting **for** his people – without
God it was a waste of time!
2) If they sinned, God would fight **against** them. If they
were a bad army, he would summon Nebuchadnezzar of
Babylon and Ashurbanipal of Assyria and others, to bring

destruction on Israel. But if Israel stayed with God, God would fight for them and make them victorious against the biggest empires of the world.

3) On a very few occasions, God would fight **through** them. He would certainly use their praise as weapons, but he even used their swords a little too!

Now if we translate these three things into the New Testament, we can still say that God will fight for us – that is our confidence! That is why we can be patient with him. We do not have to try and force his hand because we can be sure that ultimately he will vindicate us. Secondly, God will fight against the church if it is sinful and rebellious – that has happened repeatedly through church history. The decimation of the church, very often, is because of its corruption. God has brought parts of it down and raised up new movements and leaders. Thirdly, there is still a sense in which God will use us as his instrument in warfare, but excluding the use of the sword. He will use us to exert his power into situations – that is our spiritual warfare. God broke into Peter's prison cell, when the church appealed to him, and sent an angel to open the door – that is spiritual warfare; that is the church fighting in prayer to see God's power transform a situation – and Peter walked out free! It is also spiritual warfare when Jesus or his disciples command a demon to leave someone, which happens numerous times in the New Testament. So God fights in all the ways he would have done in the Old Testament with the exception of using violence itself. Power can be brought to bear on situations: Jesus is using power and spiritual warfare as he walks through the crowd and avoids being executed and thrown over the precipice. There are times when the church will walk fearless through the angry crowd because the power of God is working for us and protecting us.

Now, that is Holy War in its three elements: God fights for us, God fights against us and God fights through us. All of these are to continue, I believe, in these last days. We have been promised that we will do not only the works that Jesus did, but greater works. There are not many greater works in the New Testament, although there are some. I think Peter's shadow falling over a person and healing them is a greater work than the healing which came through grabbing hold of Jesus' garment. Likewise, when Paul's sweatband was removed and passed around bringing healing to many people even in his absence, it seems a greater work than when Jesus healed one Centurion's slave with a word at a distance. Jesus did not get John the Baptist out of prison, but Peter was freed when the church prayed – a greater work!

When Paul says that the church will come to the full knowledge of the Son of God, or the fullness of Christ (Eph. 4:13), he implies, not only the fullness of Christ in breadth in every tribe, tongue, kindred people and nation, but also in depth. The depth of our knowledge of him will release his power much more considerably than we have yet experienced. The book of Revelation shows us that this age, or the end of the Age, is marked by two events (Rev. 11:3-6) – calling down fire and changing water to blood. This is a fairly aggressive picture. They have one body between them and so are a symbol of a significant minority of the church, also depicted by the two of the seven lampstands (v4). They are not two individuals, as is popularly taught. I do not know in detail what these symbols mean, but I think we will know when such things happen – and I do believe that it reinforces the place for spiritual warfare in the church today.

Perhaps an even more provocative question, and one that requires some careful thought in the light of Old Testament Holy War, is the role of prayer in a situation of terrorist attack or other forms of violence. Should we be expecting to see bombs blowing up terrorists rather than the innocent because the church has been praying against them? Surely the church should be engaged in seeing some preventative measures put in place through their prayers, so that evil is restrained. That is possibly more what it is to engage in 'Holy War' on a New Testament level, and I believe we should see more of it. Whatever God chooses in response to our intercession, it would, of course, be consistent with Christ's love for both victims and aggressors.

When Jesus was challenged about his Messiahship, his kingship, his reply was not, 'Yes, I am afraid that is who I am, is that alright with you?' Our Lord is nothing but provocative in these situations. He seems to be intent upon deliberately upsetting people! He replied even to the high priest himself, not in mealy-mouthed terms that might have saved him from some punishment, but simply, 'Yes' using his favourite name for himself, 'And you will see the Son of Man coming in the clouds and seated at the right hand of power'. True to form, Jesus presents himself, not as the Messiah, not as the King of Kings, not as the Lord of Lords, but as the Son of Man. Jesus used the title so much that eventually the people asked him 'Who is this Son of Man?' So, who is he?

# 6

# The Son of Man and His Kingdom

At the beginning we thought about two neglected subjects in the church. One is our central message of the Kingdom of God, which we are rediscovering in this book. The other is this title we hardly ever use for Jesus, intimately related to the Kingdom, 'the Son of Man'. Perhaps in recovering the Kingdom it is almost unavoidable that we are going to recover an understanding of the Son of Man as well. What does it mean that Jesus was the Son of Man? Why does he use this obscure kind of terminology? Why pick a title that is so meaningless to so many people, when he could have used 'Son of God', 'Emmanuel' or 'Jahweh' and so on?

I have already given an indication that the reason lies partly in the politics of the day, and the politics of the Kingdom. Jesus called himself 'Son of Man' so that people would understand the Messiah *his* way, rather than according to popular conception. His way was couched in a term which the Jews did not apply directly to the Messiah. We may find some manuscripts and Dead Sea Scrolls that tend towards this meaning, but as far as we can tell the Son of Man was not a title that was commonly used for the Messiah. Yet Jesus picks it up and uses it, since any other term he might have chosen would have already been used. He particularly chooses a name that is unknown.

Jesus says in Matthew's gospel, 'You will see the Son of Man coming in His Kingdom,' slightly changing the words from the vision in Daniel 7 where the Son of Man is seen to be coming 'in the clouds' (Mk. 13:26). Daniel's vision is the background for understanding Jesus and his message. There are at least eight references to Daniel 7 in Matthew's gospel alone. He is using Daniel 7, calling himself 'the Son of Man' and talking about 'his Kingdom'. The book of Daniel is, therefore, very important in Jesus' self-understanding and revelation. We need to first consider Daniel 7 before moving on to other passages in this book. In the first eight verses, four kingdoms are depicted. Kings and kingdoms are almost identifiable with each other and are represented by wild animals – grotesque and bizarre animals which either bring fear or laughter because they are so stupid-looking. How on earth do you function with four heads or ten horns?! But the time comes when Daniel says:

Then I kept looking because of the sound of the boastful words which the horn was speaking; I kept looking until the beast was slain, and its body was destroyed and given to the burning fire. As for the rest of the beasts, their dominion was taken away, but an extension of life was granted to them for an appointed period of time.

I kept looking in the night visions,
And behold, with the clouds of heaven
One like a Son of Man was coming.
And He came up to the Ancient of Days

And was presented before Him.
And to Him was given dominion,
Glory and a kingdom,
That all the peoples, nations, and men of every language
Might serve Him.
His dominion is an everlasting dominion
Which will not pass away;
And His kingdom is one
Which will not be destroyed.

You can see why the high priest was upset when he heard Jesus referring to himself in this manner (Mk. 14:61-63)! He was claiming to be the Son of Man, defeating those who opposed him and receiving their authority for himself from the Ancient of Days.

The eternity of the Kingdom of the Son of Man and his exclusive authority is put in contrast to the wild animals and their kingdoms. In this way the Son of Man can be understood as a type of Adam, a designation for humanity:

What is man that You take thought of him,
And the *son of man* that You care for him?
Yet You have made him a little lower than God,
And You crown him with glory and majesty!
You make him to rule over the works of Your hands;
You have put all things under his feet...

(Ps. 8:4-6)

In Hebrew poetry, 'man' and 'Son of Man' are equivalents. 'You have put all things under his feet' refers to God's command to Adam who was told to subdue all things and have dominion over the animals. So, 'Man', 'Son of Man', Adam and the dominion over the animals are concepts that take us back to Genesis 1. In the beginning, the Spirit moved over the surface of the deep and out of it came the earth and then its beasts. Daniel 7:2-3 tells us that the beasts came forth from the sea: 'I was looking in my vision by night and behold four winds of heaven were stirring up the great sea'. There is a clear allusion here to Adam and his dominion over the earth and over the animals. But this time, the angel interprets to us in verse 17, the beasts are empires of men who have become bestial without God, hence their empires look like wild and crazy animals. How would the kingdoms of Nebuchadnezzar or Cyrus and Alexander ever be controlled and subdued? When would the true and everlasting kingdom arise, when would the kingdom of God appear?

Daniel says, 'And in the night visions I saw one like a Son of Man'. Here comes not just a man, not just Adam, but the second man, or the last Adam, to take the kingdoms and subdue them. He would quell the animal libidos that cause men to make empires that only express base animal life instead of human. Jesus is the great human, the new human, the new humanity, the Son of Man who appears in the heavens. He has access right to the throne of the Ancient of Days and a Kingdom is given to him so that he should have dominion over all the animals and so that all the earth should be subject to him, just as it should have been to Adam. His Kingdom is an everlasting Kingdom and it will never be destroyed.

We can see how excited a man like Daniel, a prime minister in Babylon, would have been. He would have seen all the terrible things that tyrants, emperors and dictators had done, subduing men and women so that they looked like animals instead of sons of God. All of this is going to be banished as *the* true man, the Son of Man, appears. The Son of Man takes all these empires and rules over them. Some of them have a continued existence under his feet; others disappear completely.

This vision of Daniel's is a wonderful picture that Jesus uses prolifically in the New Testament. He is the Son of Man – a mysterious figure, never exactly identified with the Messiah. There is terrific revelation in Jesus' use of the term 'Son of Man'. Perhaps most immediately evident in Daniel 7 is the promise of the King who was to come and reign in the Kingdom. If a Jewish boy or girl had been taught these Scriptures well in the synagogue (they usually only taught the boys), and then had heard Jesus uniquely declare himself the Son of Man, they would have been amazed and overwhelmed that this person had really come.

But before we look more closely at the term, 'Son of Man', I want us to think about the three different occurrences of the related word 'Kingdom' in the first six chapters of Daniel. Firstly, in Daniel 2:44-45:

And in the days of those kings the God of heaven will set up a **kingdom** which will never be destroyed, and that **kingdom** will not be left for another people; it will crush and put an end to all these **kingdoms**, but it will itself endure forever. Inasmuch as you saw that a stone was cut out of the mountain without hands and that it crushed the iron, the bronze, the clay, the silver and the gold, the great God has made known to the king what will take place in the future; so the dream is true, and its interpretation is trustworthy.

Most interpreters popularly apply verses 44-45 to the Second Coming where the stone destroying the image is like the sudden impact of Jesus' return breaking into the earth and shattering the kingdoms of this world. However, I think that this part of the imagery applies to the incarnation, Jesus breaking into humanity at his birth, then his proclamation which shook the rulers and authorities in heaven and on earth in his later years: 'the Kingdom of Heaven is at hand!' But the latter part of the vision – the mountain that shall fill the whole earth – that certainly anticipates the Second Coming, when all the kingdoms of this earth have been blown apart and Christ shall fill all things (Eph. 4:10). If we put both parts of the interpretation together, the picture shows us how the Kingdom of God is in the process of taking over the whole of the earth, so that the kingdoms of this world shall become the Kingdom of our God and his Christ.

Secondly, if we look at Daniel 4:3, Nebuchadnezzar says 'How great are His signs, and how mighty are His wonders! His **Kingdom** is an everlasting **Kingdom**, and His dominion is from generation to generation...' and he goes onto speak about God reigning in the kingdoms of men:

...for His dominion is an everlasting dominion, and His **Kingdom** endures from generation to generation. And all the

> inhabitants of the earth are accounted as nothing, but He does according to His will in the host of heaven and among the inhabitants of earth; and no one can ward off His hand or say to Him, 'What have You done?'
>
> (Dan. 4:3 and 34-35).

Nebuchadnezzar had become sick in the head and was crawling around like an animal, until he was mercifully restored and God gave him his kingdom back. So in these verses, he is talking about how God can work out the purposes of his kingdom in the midst of the kingdoms of men. This is a concept of the Kingdom which is not a dramatic breaking-in and filling up the earth. It is the Kingdom still at a distance. It is the Kingdom in terms of the everlasting reign of God, more the sovereignty of God approach. God works in all things according to the counsel of his Will from the outside because his Kingdom is perfect in the Heavens but it is not practised perfectly here on earth. He can over-rule even the sin of man. Earlier we used the analogy of a master chess player who keeps manoeuvring the pieces to bring about the ultimate end of checkmate. That is the everlasting eternal Kingdom that runs from Genesis through to Revelation, but it is external to the immediacy of what is going on here on the earth.

What Jesus means when he says 'the Kingdom of Heaven is at hand' is that this kingdom has broken into earthly events. Nebuchadnezzar, in Daniel 4, is not talking about the everlasting Kingdom breaking in. The everlasting Kingdom is that which is external to space but overrules through madness, through natural order, through cause and effect, through winds and rains to get his Will done as he works in all things according to the counsel of his Will. It is not the breaking in that takes place at the Second Coming and dominates the earth.

Neither is it the kingdom as it is reflected in Daniel 6:26-27, and this is a third aspect of the Kingdom found in these opening chapters:

> I make a decree that in all the dominion of my Kingdom men are to fear and tremble before the God of Daniel; for He is the living God and enduring forever, and His **Kingdom** is one which will not be destroyed, and His dominion will be forever. He delivers and rescues and performs signs and wonders in heaven and on earth, who has also delivered Daniel from the power of the lions.

At that moment when, according to nature, the lions should have chewed Daniel up, God broke in and put his hand over the lions' mouths and, with signs and wonders and interventions, the Kingdom had come for Daniel. This is the immediate and invasive kingdom of God which interrupts our earthly lives to bring in something of heaven.

Thus, three distinct aspects of the Kingdom are here discernible. Daniel 2 is the final break-in of the rule of God throughout the Universe that the Second Coming will complete, when the kingdoms of this world will become the Kingdom of our God and His Christ. Daniel 6 is the immediate breaking in today with signs and wonders by the power of the Holy Spirit, as we pray 'Your Kingdom come!' and ask God to come into a situation and get his Will done on earth as it is in Heaven. Finally, arching and over-arching both of those Kingdom views, Daniel 4 is the reign of God as King over the universe, working in all things according to the counsel of his Will for the purposes of his everlasting and heavenly kingdom. That gives us a total picture of the Kingdom of God.

When we pray 'Your Kingdom come!', we are not praying for the eternal reign of God to continue – that happens whether we like it or not, it doesn't matter how much we pray about it! Rather, we are praying for the intervention of the Holy Spirit or angels to break in, act supernaturally, and bring signs and wonders and deliverance. Or if not, we are praying for the end when Jesus will come again and establish the kingdom of God on the earth in all its finality. Similarly, when Jesus says 'the Kingdom of God is at hand', he is referring to the latter two things and not to the eternal Kingdom that has always been there. The Kingdom message which Jesus preached is not 'God is working in all things and the mills of God grind slowly but surely...', it is 'God come now and do something! Heal the sick and deliver the demoniacs! Bring down corrupt governments and get your Will done on Herod!'

So there is the Kingdom now, there is the Kingdom to come and there is the Kingdom which is outside space all the time.

In order to understand the instrument that brings Jesus' Kingdom in, we need to look again into Daniel 7 and unpack Jesus' use of his favourite title, 'Son of Man'. We will do this by looking at the title in the light of eight pairs of alternatives.

## 1) Human or Divine?

As we see it in the text, it is obvious that the Son of Man must be human . As Daniel looks at this vision, he sees the figure of a man emerging in stark contrast to the figures of the beasts that were previously prevailing. The man, the last Adam, the Second Man (to use Pauline terminology[3]) had come to reign over the empires and kingdoms of the world. He is human, but we are given reason to pause for a minute and think again. Daniel says he is only *like* a Son of Man. If the Son of Man is only 'like' a Son of Man, then perhaps he is really something different.

We are told of only one other who is *like* a human being, and that is God who made men and women in his own likeness. 'Let us make man in our own image' (Gen. 1:26). Male and female he created them. If then, this figure is only 'like' a Son of Man and yet is not a Son of Man full stop, then the Scripture not only implies but almost demands that he must be divine.

The divinity of the Son of Man is equally driven to our consciousness because we are told he comes in the clouds. The clouds are the clothing of God. When God goes out in public he needs to be clothed, just like you do when you go out in public. The only difference is that you are seen if you are not clothed, whereas God is not seen because he is invisible. If he does not put on his 'cloudy' clothes, you do not know that he is there. He rides upon the cherubim and he comes in the clouds – that is the picture of the tangible, conscious and experiential presence of God which occurs time and again in the Old Testament: the pillar of cloud that led the people of Israel out of Egypt, the clouds of incense that covered the mercy seat in the holy place of the tent of meeting. The God who is everywhere is seen to be somewhere when he puts on his clothes.

Daniel sees the Son of Man wrapped in clouds. It would seem that he is wearing God's clothes. My son, and even my two daughters, would you believe it, all had spates of wearing their father's clothes. They seemed to think they had a right to invade my drawers and steal my shirts (my daughters even stole my waistcoats − daughters in waistcoats! It was never done in my day...). They think that because they are the children of the father, they can wear their father's clothes. Here, the Son of Man comes wearing God's clothes. He must be in a relationship with him somehow.

Daniel 7:14 says, '...that all the peoples, nations and men of every language might serve Him'. This service is not simply as a slave might serve his master, but it implies *worshipful* service[4]. Who is allowed to be served worshipfully other than God? That was Jesus' temptation in the wilderness, when he refused to worship Satan, saying 'It is written, "You shall worship the Lord your God and serve him only"' (Lk. 4:8). The nations in the vision are worshipping the Son of Man and serving him as God.

The New Testament picture of the Son of Man goes beyond Daniel 7:13 and depicts him as so close to the Ancient of Days that he not only wears his cloudy clothes, but he also wears his hair. He wears the wig of the Ancient of Days! Revelation 1 says 'I saw the Son of Man and His hair was white as wool'. Revelation 1:14 describes the

Ancient of Days thus: 'His vesture was like white snow, and the hair of His head like pure wool'. The Ancient of Days and the Son of Man must be so closely associated that there is a unity, a oneness about them, even if the Old Testament does not fully define it in trinitarian terms.

The Son of Man in the Old Testament already contains the seeds that grow logically into the New Testament conclusion that the one *like* the Son of Man is divine. He is both divine *and* human. So, when Jesus called himself 'the Son of Man', he was asserting his divinity and his humanity. Any Jew who had meditated on this text of Scripture with the help of the Holy Spirit would have begun to realise that they were dealing with someone who was divine as well as human, and would have moved closer to the truth of who Jesus was.

## 2) Singular or Plural?

Another conundrum over which theologians have puzzled is the question of whether 'Son of Man' describes an individual or a group of people. In a sense, we have already begun to answer that question. If we can see a parallel with Adam in the Second Man, the Son of Man, then of course, naturally when we talk about Adam (man) we are also talking about the whole of humanity (mankind). Hidden in the one unique individual Adam is a whole human race. Therefore, if the Son of Man is taking over Adam's role in subduing the earth and ruling the animals, we should not be surprised if we find that he is both singular and plural, individual and corporate. Daniel says '**one** like the Son of Man was coming', '**He** came', 'And to **Him** was given', 'that might serve **Him**' – these are all singular. Then, when you get towards the end of this passage, we find 'And he will speak out against the Most High and wear down **the saints** of the Highest One', 'then the sovereignty, the dominion, and the greatness of all the kingdoms under the whole heaven will be given to **the people of the saints** of the Highest One'. Moreover, in verse 18 the angel interprets the whole vision to Daniel, saying 'But **the saints** of the Highest One will receive the Kingdom and possess the Kingdom forever, for all ages to come.' So, the Son of Man who receives the Kingdom in verse 14 has now become the saints who receive the Kingdom in verse 18.

The Son of Man has his Kingdom, but at the same time it is the Kingdom belonging to the people of the saints of the Most High. This Son of Man is both individual and corporate because, just like Adam had a whole human race in him, so Jesus has a whole new humanity in him. That is why he gave us bread and said, 'This is My Body for you' – we are what we eat, and when we eat the bread, we eat his Body and we become a part of his Body ourselves. Therefore we are the Body of Christ and a whole host of us is contained in that one Body of the Son of Man. When Jesus told the Jews that he was the Son of Man, he was actually saying that there was a whole new human race in him. These are the saints of the Highest One, and they constitute a whole new type of humanity.

That is why when Paul uses the word 'Christ' in 1 Corinthians 12, he means it in a corporate sense: 'Just as the body has eyes and ears and hands and feet, so also is the Christ'. He is not referring to Jesus as an individual, he is referring to the Body of Jesus. Most bodies have the same name as their heads! So, we share the name 'Christ' because our head has got the name 'Christ'. My body has got the name Roger Forster because my head has. If you were to punch me in the body and then say, 'It's alright, I am not punching you, I am just punching your body!' I would still complain bitterly and probably punch you back, because my head and my body are the same!

So it is with the Body of Christ. When the apostle Paul was called Saul, and was destroying the Body of believers, Jesus said, 'Saul, Saul why do you persecute Me?' Paul might have said, 'But I am not persecuting you, you're dead and buried or in heaven or hell or somewhere – but you are certainly not the people I am beating up!' And Jesus would say, 'I am in my people, so much so that they are my body and what you do to them you do to me!'[5] The relationship between the Son of Man and all the little sons of men, the relationship between Adam and all the children of the earth, the relationship between the Second Man, or the last Adam with all human beings is as an individual and also corporate at the same time. This is why this title is so exciting. No wonder Jesus used it! I would suggest that the Son of Man is the richest concept that Jesus ever applied to himself. It means that he is thoroughly human, yet totally divine. It means the individual Jesus and it means the whole new humanity, the body of people hidden within him. All these concepts are already there in the text of Daniel 7.

## 3) King or Priest?

There is yet another pair of contrasting ideas in Daniel's 'Son of Man'. When it describes 'the Son of Man coming in the clouds of Heaven' and 'taking a Kingdom', he primarily looks like a King. If the Son of Man takes the Kingdom he must be a King, and therefore a Messiah. But is he only a King? It was incumbent upon the Jews that the king and the priest were two separate offices. Yet the picture of the Son of Man here also looks like a priest because he is surrounded by clouds. We have already noted that clouds in the Psalms, in the Law and in some of the minor prophets indicate the clothing of God; they indicate when God is around. However, on the Day of Atonement, the high priest also covered himself with clouds, clouds of incense to be exact. He lit the incense, enveloped himself in the clouds that billowed from it and made sure that every bit of him was hidden, because if he came without the clouds into the Holy Place, it was said, 'You will surely die'. He would enter into the Holy Place, the clouds of incense a symbol of God's expected presence, and if God was still manifesting himself to his people, then the Shekinah cloud of God's glory would descend on the Holy Place. The clouds of God would intermingle with the clouds of man and become one around the high priest. This ritual would happen every year until the time of Jesus.

When Jesus stood before the high priest and was urged 'I adjure You by the living God that You tell us whether You are the Christ, the Son of God!' (Mt. 26:63), he was being asked, 'Are you the Messiah, the Anointed One?' 'Christ',

'Messiah' and 'Anointed' are all the same word. One anointed high priest was speaking to another anointed high priest. One of them is anointed with oil, the other with the Holy Spirit. They were both 'Christs' in the technical sense of the word, for they both hold the office of an anointed one. Jesus replied with echoes of Daniel 7: 'I am; and you shall see the Son of Man sitting at the right hand of Power, and coming with the clouds of Heaven' (Mk. 14:62). But in Daniel 7, the priestly Son of Man is not coming down to earth, but going up to the Ancient of Days, and Jesus adds that he even sits down at the right hand of power. This would have appalled the high priest; to sit down at the right hand of power is to sit on God's throne! But the high priest would see the evidence that Jesus had been enthroned on the very throne of God and the power of God being released.

In the ensuing experiences, culminating in AD70, when the high priest and his Temple were removed, the destruction was evidence that the old age had finished and the new age had begun. Jesus was reigning from the throne. He who had been executed and rejected was now vindicated and he was coming in his Kingdom. In fact, Jesus had promised some of his disciples: 'Some of you standing here will not taste of death *until* you see the Son of Man coming in His power and great glory'. The word 'until' indicates that Jesus thought they would taste death afterwards, so he could not possibly be referring to the Second Coming. He was looking forward to when Jerusalem would be destroyed and all the things that were opposing Jesus, the Law, the Temple, the high priesthood and all the authorities in Israel, were all demonstrated by God to be finished. This would be Jesus coming in great power and glory.

Jesus was called a Priest after the order of Melchizedek (Heb. 5:6,10). Melchizedek was both a King and a Priest; he was King of Salem (which means 'Righteousness'), but he was also a Priest of God Most High. The two offices that were separated in Israel and never allowed to coincide were brought together in Jesus, as prophesied by Daniel in the kingly, priestly Son of Man.

## 4) Jew or Gentile?

The Son of Man is first a Jewish figure. Psalm 80 talks about the Jewish people, their exile and the judgement that had fallen upon their land. God goes on to say that he has the Man of his right hand, the Son, the Vine and the Son of Man, whom he has made strong for himself, and he is quite clearly referring to Israel – the true Israel, the Israel that is coming out of the exile:

> O God of hosts, turn again now, we beseech Thee;
> Look down from heaven and see, and take care of **this vine**,
> Even the shoot which Thy right hand has planted,
> And on **the son** whom Thou hast strengthened for Thyself.
> It is burned with fire, it is cut down;
> They perish at the rebuke of Thy countenance.
> Let Thy hand be upon **the man of Thy right hand**,
> Upon **the son of man** whom Thou didst make strong for Thyself.

Then we shall not turn back from Thee;
Revive us, and we will call upon Thy name.

(Ps.80:14–18)

The 'Son of Man' here is simply a way of referring to the
ideal Israel. The verses describe God bringing Israel back
and strengthening them after they had been burnt, attacked
and taken into exile. Jesus, of course, is the fulfilment of all
of Israel as the True Vine (Jn. 15:1). At one time, Israel was
just one man, Jacob, and from him there came thousands.
But in Jesus Israel becomes one again[6]. He sums up the
whole of Israel in his own being. He is the perfect and pure
Israel – perfect for the judgements in consequence of Israel's
broken covenant, for Jesus bore that curse in his own being
on the cross, and also perfect for the ideal obedience
that Israel, the Son of God, should have fulfilled. Jesus perfectly fulfils the Son of God and the Son of Man.

The Son of Man is Israel, and therefore Jewish, but Psalm
8 uses the 'Son of Man' to represent the totality of humanity. It speaks of all the sons of Adam, not just one Israel:

O Lord, our Lord, how majestic is your name in **all the earth!**
What is man, that Thou dost take thought of him?
And the **son of man**, that Thou dost care for him?
…You make him to **rule over the works of your hands**,
You have put **all things under his feet**.

(Ps.8:4 and 6)

These phrases in Psalm 8 use 'the Son of Man' to speak of the
whole of humanity and their Adamic role of ruling over the

earth. In Psalm 80, 'the Son of Man' represents Jewish humanity exclusively, for this people was the chosen vehicle of God's salvation for all the world. The Son of Man sums up both 'Jewishness' and 'Gentileness'. In the Messiah there is neither Jew nor Greek because both are present and they are one. It is thrilling to extrapolate from Daniel 7 that the Son of Man title embraces all of humanity as well as all of God's intentions for Israel. That is why Ephesians 3:6 says that Jew and Gentile have been 'concorporated', literally 'together-bodied', in Christ. The Son of Man is one entity, one humanity.

The Son of Man is both Jewish and Gentile, human and divine, individual and corporate, King and Priest.

## 5) Suffering or Reigning?

Similarly, we need to ask whether the picture of the church in Daniel 7 is that of a suffering or reigning church. Let us look carefully at verses 22, 25 and 27:

> He will **speak out against** the Most High and **wear down** the saints of the Highest One, and he will intend to make alterations in times and in law; and they will be **given into his hand** for a time, times, and half a time… (v25)

> Then the **sovereignty**, the dominion and the greatness of all the kingdoms under the whole heaven **will be given to the people of the saints** of the Highest One; His kingdom will be an everlasting kingdom, and all the dominions will serve and obey Him. (v27)

...judgment was passed in favor of the saints of the Highest One, and the time arrived when **the saints took possession** of the kingdom. (v22)

The fact is that the saints are suffering and being persecuted *at the same time* as they have been given the Kingdom. The passage says that the Kingdom will be forever and ever and the beast and the little horn will be put down. But it does seem that the picture is presenting that a persecuted church will possess the Kingdom. The phrase 'saints of the Most High' is preferably translated as 'saints of the high places'. It sounds like an anticipation of Ephesians 2:6 which talks about the saints who are made to sit in heavenly places and who have authority in this age.

One day the suffering will cease and only the reigning will continue, but at the moment the church must reign in life by one man, Christ Jesus. Whenever we exert the Kingdom of God by the power of the Holy Spirit, we are reigning in situations. When we cast out demons we bring in the Kingdom of God (Mt. 12:28). When we heal the sick Jesus says, 'the Kingdom of God has drawn near' (Lk. 10:9). So, we reign and we bring the Kingdom, even though we are suffering. When Jesus says 'Saul, Saul, why do you persecute Me?' he is the Son of Man still suffering. We have a picture here of the suffering church reigning, because both things actually happen on earth in this age. Both suffering and reigning have begun now, although only one will last for eternity. Praise the Lord!

## 6) Heavenly or Earthly?

Closely connected with suffering and reigning is the question of whether the Son of Man is in the heavens or on the
earth. We have already seen that he is being persecuted on
the earth in the body of his saints, but in verse 18 the angel
speaks to Daniel about 'the saints of the Highest One', or as
we have seen, it could be translated 'the Holy Ones of the
high places'. The 'Highest One' is a less probable understanding, since there is another name for God earlier in
verse 25: the 'Most High', (which is a different word in
Hebrew). 'But the saints of the high places will receive the
kingdom' – they have seen the Son of Man in the heavens,
while on the other hand, the beasts are running around on
the earth. These saints, therefore, belong to the heavens.
These holy ones sit in the heavenly places, we would say in
Pauline terms (Eph. 2:5).

But at the same time, as we have seen, they are being persecuted; they are there on the earth, experiencing earthly
trials. So are they a heavenly people or an earthly people?
They are both!   They are on earth and they are in heaven.
They sit in heavenly places in Christ Jesus but they are still
praying 'Your Kingdom come, Your Will be done on earth!'
They are still fulfilling God's purposes in being the meek
who inherit the earth. Just as the Son of Man is both heavenly and earthly, so his Body is also both heavenly and
earthly. In the new heaven and the new earth, we will need
a Son of Man who is both heavenly and earthly so that he
can look after both. Likewise, we need to be a bit of both,
so that we can reign with him in the Age to come.

I don't want the earth to disappear. Some people are always longing to be heading off to heaven, they don't seem to like it much down here! But I am not all that keen just to depart. While we are on earth we can be praying for God's Will to be done on it as it is in heaven. We can be bringing heaven to earth. Jesus began the process by becoming the Word made flesh, abiding in us (Jn. 14), fleshing out heaven in our earthly existence. We are looking forward to the time when Jesus will return to earth to complete what he began, and to complete it in cooperation with us was always his intention. When God told Adam to go and fill up the earth, the idea was to fill the whole earth with his glory. It is now the church's job to continue that by taking the image of the new man dwelling inside us by the Holy Spirit, and going into all the earth to make disciples of Christ.

## 7) Ascension or Second Coming?

Is this vision of the Son of Man a picture of the Ascension or the Second Coming? We can see elements of both. The 'Son of Man coming in the clouds' is on his way to meet the Ancient of Days, not coming to the earth. This is a picture of the Ascension, Jesus going back to the Father and being assimilated back in relationship to him so that in Revelation 1 he even has the white hair of the Father on him. But Daniel 7:11 talks about the destruction of the horn and the beast, and verse 14 says that the reign of the Son of Man goes on forever and ever. This must surely be a picture of Jesus coming to utterly destroy the antichrist and Satan 'with the brightness of his appearing and the breath of his lips' (2 Thes. 2:8). So, the Second Coming is also included in the vision (c.f. also 1 Thes. 4:13-18 and Acts 1:9-11).

### 8) *Judgement* For *or Judgement* Against?

Finally, there is another beautiful little touch in this 'Son of Man' passage which is worth pointing out: '...the Ancient of Days came, and judgement **was passed in favour of** the saints of the Highest One, and the time arrived when the saints took possession of the Kingdom' (Dan. 7:22). The phrase translated 'passed in favour of' is literally '**given for**'. It sounds at first as though the verse is saying that judgement was given for them in their favour, in the sense that it was to their advantage. But the Hebrew preposition also allows that it could be translated 'judgement was **given to** them', which could mean that they received a guilty verdict. Were the saints actually condemned at that point, or were they acquitted and judgement handed over to them for them to exercise? The following verses show that the judgement must have worked ultimately in their favour, because they reigned forever and ever. But is this judgement the judgement of the cross or the judgement at the Second Coming? Again we find that both ideas are contained in the concept, we do not have to make a choice between the two.

When Jesus went to Calvary, he said 'Now is the judgement of this world! Now shall the Prince of this world be cast out!' (Jn. 12:31), and in that moment on the cross, the world and all the authority and kingdom of Satan was judged. But the judgement of the world also includes us, because we were judged in that moment. Our sin was judged, our rebellion, our service to Satan was judged; there was a condemnation order written over the house of the devil – 'this house is condemned – keep out!' So our judgement happened in Christ on the cross: as we confess our sin and God agrees with us saying 'You are a sinner, you deserve to die', we die in Jesus. But then we rise up into resurrection life with him, having followed him through death and judgement and out the other side. If we have been through judgement and passed from death to life, we will be free from the final judgement. The judgement has been passed in our favour and we enjoy the benefits of it.

But then the next moment God says to us, 'Now the world has been judged, you go and rescue it from the enemy's hands and cast out the prince of this world; go and claim it back for God!' Judgement is given to us to go and see the devil cast out of all the areas that he has taken illicitly for his own. This judgement culminates in the Second Coming, when Jesus comes and those who have not accepted freedom in Christ will be judged. Amazingly, we will judge with him. We are 'saviours on Mount Zion' (Obad. 1:21). We are those who judge angels (1 Cor. 6:3). We are those who judge the world (1 Cor. 6:2). We will be there when he looks at the nations and says, 'As much as you have done for *these my brothers*', referring to us, and we will reply, 'Yes, this is right, this one did, this one did not' (Mt. 25:40). Isn't it incredible? This judgement, which is given to the saints, was given in the very same moment

when we received our judgement. As we were judged as
sinners, we were given the judgement to be judges. Those
who refuse to accept that they deserve to be judged will
never gain the right to judge others. Those who say 'I
deserve to be judged and I have died in Christ' will live to
execute judgement and to reign with him forever and ever.

So in that one verse Daniel 7:22, the Son of Man brings
together both the concept of Calvary and the Second
Coming, of the judgment that has passed and the judgment
that is yet to come. The Son of Man is both human and
divine. The Son of Man is an individual but also incorporates the saints of the high places. The Son of Man is the
anointed King, because he is taking a Kingdom, but he is
also the anointed High Priest who comes in the clouds and
makes intercession for us. The Son of Man is both Jewish
and Gentile, for they are concorporated in one body. The
Son of Man is both suffering and reigning at the same time.
The Son of Man is both in heaven and on earth. The Son
of Man was judged on the cross, and was given judgement
over the nations.

I do not think there is a richer title for Jesus in the whole
of the Bible than the one that he exclusively uses – Son of
Man. The king and his kingdom, the crucifixion, the
Second Coming, the judgement of the nations, the Church,
the new heaven and the new earth, Jesus' present ministry
and his future glory are all wrapped up in this wonderful
title, just waiting to be elicited and extracted with the help
of the Holy Spirit breathing through Scripture and writing
it into our hearts and lives.

# 7

# The Fruit of the Kingdom – The Sermon on the Mount

As the end of the Age draws near and we grow into the fullness of Christ (Eph. 5:13), we can begin to grasp the depth of the title, 'Son of Man' and also get a grip on the message of the Kingdom that we are to take into the world. Now the *result* of the message is to bring forth fruit.

Jesus' warning to Israel was that the Kingdom would be taken from it. The Kingdom had been presented to Israel in the presence and activity of Jesus in the Holy Spirit. 'If I, by the finger of God, cast out demons, be it known to you that the Kingdom of God has come upon you' (Lk. 11:20). Israel had been experiencing God's Kingdom in Jesus, and through the apostles who were told to heal the sick and declare, 'the Kingdom of God has come near you!' But the warning was that as far as the nation was concerned, the Kingdom would be removed from it. 'The Kingdom will be removed from you and given to another who will bring forth the fruit of the Kingdom' (Mt. 21:43). It is quite a biblical concept that the Kingdom can be taken away from us. The Kingdom is not something which is statutorily or irremovably given. The Kingdom is a dynamic principle, it is reigning and bringing the reign of God to bear upon the earth.

Therefore, there is surely the possibility that within the church we could experience the same thing as Israel did. We could be a section of the church from which the Kingdom is removed. Revivals which have arisen and subsided throughout history could be understood in terms of the Kingdom being given or taken away. If the church, or bits of the church, like Israel, repudiate or misuse the privilege of the Kingdom, then it will be given to others. I think this is one way of understanding what happens in revival. God gives people the Kingdom and they move into it until they become proud and self-centred and try to use the Kingdom for their own ends. Then God takes it away and gives it to somebody else. That is one reason why so many denominations exist in the Church. Often, a new denomination will arise out of a new movement of the Spirit and that gives them a new emphasis. The day then eventually comes when the freshness and flexibility of the new movement begins to harden off into a more calcified form. It needs to be broken up or softened again, because the people lost touch with the Kingdom, and God moved on and gave it to another group of overcomers who could continue with it.

That is obviously speculating out of the Scriptures, to some degree, but what is clear is that the Kingdom was removed from a certain group of people – a nation – and that it was given to a 'nation' that would bring forth the fruit of it, namely, the early church. The fruit of the Kingdom is an important subject for reflection. What is the fruit of the Kingdom, in other words, what are the effects of putting it into practice? Let us look first at Matthew 4:17:

> From that time Jesus began to preach and say 'Repent, for the Kingdom of Heaven is at hand.' Walking by the Sea of Galilee, he calls some fisherman – Peter, Andrew, James and John – and tells them to follow him and he will make them fishers of men. That was the people of the Kingdom coming into being. The Kingdom needs an instrument through which to work.

Then Jesus starts the work of the Kingdom as he preaches and heals the sick (Mt. 4:23). We have evangelism in its three aspects: **Proclamation** evangelism 'Jesus was going throughout all Galilee, teaching in their synagogues and proclaiming the Gospel of the Kingdom' (Mt. 4:23); **Power** evangelism 'And they brought to him all who were ill, those suffering with various diseases and pains, demoniacs, epileptics, paralytics; and he healed them' (Mt. 4:24); **Presence** evangelism 'The people who were sitting in darkness saw a great light – and upon them a light dawned' (Mt. 4:16). Jesus had just moved from Nazareth to Capernaum and in so doing, he fulfilled the prophetic Scripture that said 'the light would shine in Zebulon and Naphtali' (Is. 9:1). This is presence evangelism – the very presence of God's people in a society, a worshipping community who do the acts of Jesus, washing feet, feeding the poor, healing the sick and so on. The presence of God's people shines a light on society by the supernatural power of the Spirit. Thus Jesus introduces to us a comprehensive approach to evangelism in all its dimensions.

The Kingdom work was very successful: 'Great multitudes followed Him from Galilee and Decapolis and Jerusalem and Judea and from beyond the Jordan' (Mt. 4:25). The people of the Kingdom, that is Peter, James, John and Andrew, are following Jesus closely to see what he will do next. Matthew 5:1 says that when Jesus saw the multitudes he immediately rushed out into the crowd, laid hands on all the sick, worked for 24 hours a day until he single-handedly got through them all and finally collapsed with a nervous breakdown...! No, it does not say that, but nevertheless, that is just the way that some Christians live!

Instead it says, 'And when He saw the multitudes, He went up on the mountain; and after He sat down, His disciples came to Him'. Jesus thought the best way to reach the masses in the world (today there are over 6000,000,000 of us), was to take his disciples up the mountain and to teach them, saying 'Blessed are the poor in spirit, for theirs is the Kingdom of Heaven', and so on... The Sermon on the Mount (Mt. 5:1-7:29) is the first body of teaching that Jesus addresses to his Kingdom people, the disciples, and therefore it is the first place we should look if we want to find out what is involved in bringing forth the fruit of the Kingdom.

There are eight beatitudes. The 'ninth' beatitude is not really a new beatitude it is a repetition of the last one. The eight beatitudes are clearly marked out because they all read 'Blessed are *they*'. When you get to verse 11, what is sometimes called the 'ninth' beatitude, it changes to read 'Blessed are *you*'. The shift from the third person to the second person shows Jesus beginning to address what he is saying to the disciples specifically, applying his teaching to them and making it personal. 'Blessed are *you* when people insult *you* and persecute *you* and falsely say all kinds of evil against *you* because of *me…*' The disciples did not know it, but they were being prepared to face such things for Jesus' sake. Verses 11-20 give us an exposition of the eighth beatitude (v10) 'Blessed are those who have been persecuted for the sake of righteousness'. It tells us about the persecution and the hostility that Kingdom people will meet when they seek to bring forth fruit and be salt and light in the earth and the darkness.

As we read on through the Sermon a rather beautiful pattern begins to emerge. Jesus uses a rabbinic method to continue to expound the eight beatitudes one by one in reverse order. In verses 21-26 the second exposition is of 'blessed are the peacemakers', beatitude number seven: 'You have heard the ancients say "you shall not commit murder"'. This concerns peace-making and how to be right with your brother. 'Blessed are the pure in heart' – beatitude six – is expounded in verses 27-37: 'You shall not commit adultery… You shall not make false vows…' Beatitude number five, 'Blessed are the merciful' is addressed in verses 38-42. When you get to beatitude four, 'Blessed are those who hunger and thirst after righteousness', chapter 6 warns 'Beware of practising your righteousness before men'. Whether it is a matter of prayer, fasting or tithing, the righteousness that you are practising should not be done before men. Then Matthew 6:19-34 is all about inheriting the earth and its resources, beatitude three 'the meek shall inherit the earth'. How do they inherit it? By not laying up treasures on earth, but rather seeking the Kingdom of

God. Beatitude number two is found in Matthew 7:1-6, an encouragement to those who mourn over their own sin and other people's: don't criticise and be comforted! The first beatitude 'Blessed are the poor in the Spirit, for theirs is the Kingdom of Heaven', is addressed in Matthew 7:7, because if you are poor you ask, you seek, you knock and you receive what the Father gives – bread and not a stone. Then Jesus tells us about entering the Kingdom of Heaven: 'Not everyone that says "Lord, Lord" will enter…' and we have a full exposition of verse 3, which is beatitude number one. There are all sorts of books on expounding the Sermon on the Mount, but in actual fact, the Lord has already done it for us! The Rabbinic method uses little word games, acrostics, poetry or poetic parallelism, some structure that helps you to remember the content.

The first and the last beatitudes have something in common: 'Blessed are the poor in spirit, for theirs is the *Kingdom of Heaven*' and 'Blessed are those who have been persecuted for the sake of righteousness, for theirs is the *Kingdom of Heaven*'. The Kingdom is the theme of the beatitudes – all of them, not just the first and the last. It is the comprehensive idea that holds them all together. Jesus comes preaching the Kingdom of Heaven and then he chooses his disciples and says 'The Kingdom of Heaven is at hand!' Then Jesus puts it into *your* hands, 'Yours is…' not 'Yours shall be…' The Kingdom of Heaven is ours *now*. So the people who are living in the blessing of the beatitudes are those who are living in the Kingdom of Heaven. Why is it important that the Kingdom of Heaven is ours? So that we can gloat over it? So that we can possess it? So that we can exploit it? Not at all! We have the Kingdom of Heaven put into our hands because there are so many multitudes out there that the Lord is never going to reach except through us his Body – the church. This is his idea, his instrument and method.

As a Kingdom people, the disciples are to bring forth Kingdom fruit (Mt. 21:43), but Jesus warns us that this may be a difficult process. We can see it in verses 11-12: 'Blessed are you when you are persecuted on my account...'. Why should we be persecuted? Surely Jesus wants us to be happy and blessed, that is what the beatitudes are all about, after all! But he seems to say here that we will never be happy until we are persecuted for his sake. We tend to think that 'when men cast insults at you and say all kinds of evil against you falsely', you should look miserable and sad, like a stained-glass window saint, so that everybody feels sorry for you and says 'poor thing!' and soothes your troubled breast. In this kind of condition, it might not be so bad being a saint. But Jesus says, 'Rejoice and be glad, leap up and down (Lk. 6:23) and be absolutely, thoroughly thrilled that you are being persecuted!' It is the very first thing Jesus teaches about the church. So, every time you get a hate letter (and I hope you get lots – you are not doing anything worthwhile in life unless you get a good bit of hate mail!), or you are spoken against because of your love for Jesus, for seeking to obey him, and bear fruit for him, you just praise God, leap up and down, rejoice and be glad, for your reward in heaven is great!

This first definition of the church in the New Testament describes it as the continuing line of the prophets, 'For in the same way they persecuted the prophets who were before you' (Mt. 5:12). In the Old Testament days, Moses wanted to spread his authority to others by the gift of the Spirit, so he called together his 70 elders, but two of them, Medad and Eldad, did not turn up. In spite of this, the Holy Spirit fell on all 70 of them and they all began to prophesy and demonstrate that the Spirit of God had come. Prophecy is always an indication that the Spirit of God is active. Then Joshua came rushing in and complained that Medad and Eldad were prophesying even though they hadn't bothered to come to the meeting! (It is terrible, isn't it, that people can get blessed without coming to the meetings?!) But Moses graciously says 'I wish that all of God's people were prophets!', and of course he was anticipating the day when it was going to be true.

Joel 2 takes up the same theme when it says 'I will pour out my Spirit upon **all flesh** and your sons and daughters will prophesy'. That is fulfilled at Pentecost, when the disciples are filled with the Holy Spirit and begin speaking in tongues. Tongues is a form of prophecy, and the outpouring of the Spirit enables us all to be prophetic witnesses: 'When the Spirit of God comes, you will be my witnesses, I will open your mouth and you will be able to witness to me to the ends of the earth' (Acts 1:8). Paul also encourages the prophetic calling of all the members of the church in Corinth when he says 'For you can all prophesy!' So the church, more than anything else, is a prophetic instrument in the stream of the Old Testament prophets. In the Old Testament days, most of the people were *not* prophets. There were just a very few select people that God used in this way. Today every one of us can open our mouths and the Spirit of God can use us prophetically. But, if you are prophetic, you will be persecuted – that's a promise from the Lord! 'For so they persecuted the prophets that were before you'.

If we are prophets, it means that *everything* about us is speaking out, declaring the purposes of God; the way we live, the way we talk, the way we relate together – it is all prophecy, for the people of the Kingdom are a prophetic people. It is by prophesying, whether in word or action, or altogether in a prayer meeting, that we release the activity of the Kingdom. That is why prophets invite persecution – there is a clash of Kingdoms! When Moses stands by the Red Sea and prophesies by lifting up his rod as a prophetic act, then God 'kings' it over the opposing forces that would keep the people of Israel bound up in slavery to Egypt, and they walk triumphantly through the Red Sea on dry land. That was God's prophet acting prophetically and for the first time in the Bible we read that 'God reigns' (Ex. 15:18-19). Similarly, when the Israelites marched around the walls of Jericho for seven days, (seven times on the last day), and they all blew their trumpets – that was a prophetic blast! There is no literal cause-effect relationship between the blast of the trumpet and the falling of the wall. They blew their trumpets prophetically and God acted 'kingishly' and brought the walls down. Jehoshaphat and his people worshipping on the battle field was a form of prophecy. As they sang praises to God, they stood there prophetically, defenceless apart from the Lord. But the battle was the Lord's (2 Chron. 20:15). So, the Moabites and the Ammonites and the Edomites all fought each other and the Israelites did not have to do anything else, because God had reigned on that battlefield. The church is here to prophetically unleash the Kingdom of God onto situations in just the same sort of way.

Sometimes when we talk about 'releasing the Holy Spirit' or 'releasing the Kingdom' people don't like the terminology. They think it sounds as if we have control over the Holy Spirit. Of course, no one could really believe that. All it is meant to convey is that room is being given for God to exercise his power according to his own will. We are offering our lives to be filled and used by the Holy Spirit in the situation in which we stand. In this sense, I think it is a good phrase as we seek to avoid limiting the Lord. We release the Spirit or the Kingdom by prophetic action, prophetic praise, prophetic prayer, prophetic declaration and prophetic preaching. When everything about us is prophetic, then we are releasing more and more of the activity of the Kingdom of God, which by Paul's definition is justice, joy and peace in the activity of the Holy Spirit (Rom. 14:17).

If the church does *not* act or speak prophetically, is it then surprising that we do not see much of the Kingdom and its fruit? We have to see the Kingdom of God operating and bearing fruit by acting and speaking prophetically. A part of the whole idea behind 'March for Jesus' is to get people out on the streets, speaking, acting and praising prophetically, because that is a part of getting the church working to see the Kingdom come and the power of God released. The prophetic calling of the church is something that the devil attacks again and again, because this is what is putting him out of business.

If the church is out to be a nice worshipping club, or a philosophical, debating society then it is not going to change anything. When the church starts to be prophetic, then all sorts of things happen. If this brings persecution, it is not surprising. 'You are the salt of the earth' (Mt. 5:13). When salt meets wounds and corruption it bites and stings. 'You are the light of the world' (Mt. 5:14). When light hits darkness it destroys it; there is hostility between them. That is the warfare which produces the persecution for the prophets. It is the inevitable result of being prophetic. You cannot be prophetic without being provocative. That does not mean that we go around provoking people, it means that when we go around loving everybody it will produce hostility. Love people well enough and they will either get converted or they'll hate you for it – that is the way it goes!

Jesus says, 'Rejoice, and be glad, for your reward in Heaven is great, for so they persecuted the prophets before you. You are the salt of the earth; but if the salt has become tasteless, how will it be made salty again? It is good for nothing anymore, except to be thrown out and trampled under foot by men' (Mt. 5:12-13). When the church is not prophetic, it gets thrown out and trampled under foot by men; they completely ignore it, despise it and walk over it. People won't necessarily love you for being prophetic, but they will more than likely just despise and ignore you when you are not. 'You are the light of the world, a city set on a hill cannot be hidden' (Mt. 5:14). The city set on the hill is like an anticipation of the New Jerusalem. People can look at the church, see us together, see our holy order and be amazed, thanking God and saying, 'That is how life should have always been!' God's people relate together as a community, sharing life, love and laughter, as well as all the problems and difficulties. They are a people who start to demonstrate that there is such a thing as a New Jerusalem; there is a heaven that is coming. The church is a sign to the earth that the Kingdom is coming; atheists may mock Christians with taunts of 'Pie in the sky, get ready to die!', but our city set on a hill is like the current slice which proves there is more to come.

To many Christians religion is a private thing – 'Oh, I have got a very deep and spiritual experience of God all alone by myself. I just shut myself in my home and I pull the curtains and I really do love Jesus!' Well, that is all very well, but the Lord never told us to do that, in fact he said quite the opposite. Whether we like it or not, whether we are full of English reserve or not, we must not hide away in our faith. The Lord says 'You don't light a lamp and put it under a bushel (a measure for wheat), you put it on a stand where it can give light to the whole room!' The church has to be in a place where it can be seen, because it then gives out light. If it is hidden, then it doesn't give any light. The problem is that we try to avoid persecution by hiding away or keeping our mouths shut, and we think that we can still be pleasing to God. I am sure he is pleased that there are people who love him and seek to serve him discreetly, but that is not bringing in the Kingdom.

'Let your light shine before men in such a way that they may see your good works, and glorify your Father who is in Heaven' (Mt. 5:16). It does not quite say that our good works are the light, but that our light is what enables people to see the good works. If you do a humanistic good work, without God empowering it by the Holy Spirit, then people will say what a fine fellow or a super lady you are. If you do a good work in the power of the Holy Spirit, light will shine as you do it and people will see that the good work is nothing to do with you and how brilliant you are. They will see that you are not much good for anything at all, really, but they will look at the good work and say 'You must have a marvellous father somewhere!' How do they know that? Because the light has shone. They will never glorify the Father for a good work until the light is shining. They will either thank you for it, or they will thank the Father, and if they thank the Father, then it proves that his light has been shining. So, you do the work and the Father gets the glory! That sounds a bit unfair, but really when he shines the light you know that you could never have done such good works anyway. It is his works that are coming through you, his guidance, the way he uses and leads you and gives you prophetic insight to release the Spirit through you. A church filled with the oil of the Spirit day by day is the only church who will bring forth Kingdom fruit, good works that shine with supernatural light.

That is supernatural holiness, Kingdom fruitfulness. There is nothing natural about it. In the Old Testament, God helped people to be holy, but in the New Testament he executes us and puts a whole new holy life inside us. The life that we now live in the flesh is not ours it is his, because we are crucified with Christ. It is Jesus living in you that is shining the light and everybody can see that it is the Father who has done it all because he has put the Son inside you (Gal. 2:20).

# 8

# *The Gospel of the Kingdom*

In Matthew 21:33–43 Jesus tells a parable:

> Listen to another parable. There was a landowner who planted
> a vineyard and put a wall around it and dug a wine press in it,
> and built a tower, and rented it out to vine-growers and went
> on a journey. When the harvest time approached, he sent his
> slaves to the vine-growers to receive his produce. The vine-
> growers took his slaves and beat one, and killed another, and
> stoned a third. Again he sent another group of slaves larger than
> the first; and they did the same thing to them. But afterward he
> sent his son to them, saying, 'They will respect my son'. But
> when the vine-growers saw the son, they said among them-
> selves, 'This is the heir; come, let us kill him and seize his
> inheritance . . .'
>
> Therefore I say to you, the kingdom of God will be taken
> away from you and given to a people, producing the fruit of it.

The parable tells us that there is a Kingdom and there is the
fruit of the Kingdom, which as we saw in the previous
chapter, is the impact of obedience to the Lord in salting
and lighting our society. The Christians who talk about the
Kingdom of God and emphasise the social/political impact

which the gospel should make in our communities, are not totally wrong. But sometimes they confuse the fruit of the Kingdom with the Kingdom itself. The Kingdom is the supernatural activity of the power of God. The effect that can have on the world in forming a new and beautiful society is the fruit of the Kingdom. There are many books rightly grappling with the issues of social justice, but wrongly equating taking Christian social action with bringing in the Kingdom. If you do not first have the Kingdom, you will not produce the fruit. All humanistic activity, without the power of the Holy Spirit, will come to little in the end. Our fleshly efforts not only lack effectiveness, but they also create problems for the next generation of believers to try and solve. The solutions of one generation often prove to be the problems of the next – we solve one problem by creating another, but that is not the Kingdom of God. It can be very hard for people to come to terms with this distinction when they have become so used to thinking that the Kingdom is about ameliorating our condition and raising the standards and quality of our life – the salting and lighting of society. This is the consequence of the Kingdom, rather than the Kingdom itself.

We can understand more of Jesus' Kingdom by looking at his 'gospel manifesto' at the beginning of his ministry:

And He came to Nazareth, where He had been brought up; and as was His custom, He entered the synagogue on the Sabbath, and stood up to read. And the book of the prophet Isaiah was handed to Him. And He opened the book, and found the place where it was written,

'The Spirit of the Lord is upon Me,
Because He anointed Me to preach the gospel to the poor.
He has sent Me to proclaim release to the captives,
And recovery of sight to the blind,
To set free those who are downtrodden,
To proclaim the favorable year of the Lord.'

And He closed the book, and gave it back to the attendant, and
sat down; and the eyes of all in the synagogue were fixed upon
Him.

(Lk. 4:16-20)

Every eye in the meeting was fixed on the carpenter as he
read Isaiah 58:6 and 61:1-2. It was not the young man's
learning or sophisticated erudition which riveted their
attention, for he was an artisan with no more formal education than the average Jewish boy; yet there was something
different about him. Those Scriptures, well known to every
Jew, seemed somehow alive today. Of course, they knew
that Jesus was a local home-grown lad who had caused
quite a stir elsewhere in Israel, Capernaum for instance
(Lk. 4:23). There was power in his teaching; he was healing
and casting out demons. Already reports had filtered back
to Nazareth and Jesus' fellow-villagers were basking in the
glory of it. What was it, then, that was different today?
Somehow the Scriptures just fitted him.

This young Nazarene was coming out into the public eye
with scriptural clothes which everyone could see were
made for him. They were kingly robes, moreover, as he
indicated when he spoke of the anointing upon him. He

was certainly acting like a king, declaring the manifesto of his reign – good news to the poor, freedom to prisoners incarcerated in dark dungeons and liberty to the oppressed! God's age of favour was here. It was not only that he preached these things as God's Good News of the Kingdom (c.f. Lk. 4:43) but he seemed able to effect them by the power of his proclaimed word. Three times in Luke 4:18,19 proclamation of the word is emphasised in this four-point manifesto: 'The Spirit of the Lord is upon me, because he anointed me to **preach** the gospel to the poor. He has sent me to **proclaim** release to the captives, and recovery of sight to the blind, to set free those who are downtrodden, to **proclaim** the favourable year of the Lord'.

At the start of the Christian age, Jesus came into Galilee proclaiming, 'The kingdom of God is near; repent and believe the good news!' (Mk. 1:14,15). There is no such thing as Christian evangelism that is not rooted in the ideas and context of God's Kingdom. In fact this 'evangel' is called the gospel of the Kingdom: 'And Jesus was going about in all Galilee, teaching in their synagogues, and proclaiming the gospel of the kingdom' (Lk. 4:43, Mk. 1:14–15, Mt. 4:23). If we do not understand the biblical use of the phrase the 'Kingdom of God' (or Heaven), we are unable to appreciate and imitate the evangelism that Christ brought and taught.

Some more fundamentalist 'conservative evangelicals' will say that the gospel, as presented here in Jesus' manifesto, is something which is primarily **preached**, and that was the main reason for his anointing. The preaching is mentioned three times and implied in a fourth. It is quite right, then, to say that the gospel of the Kingdom is something we must proclaim. But for some, it is nothing else. Preaching is the whole gospel. It has nothing to do with social action or charismatic gifts or healing.

On the other hand, there are the charismatics, the Pentecostals and the Third Wavers who say that the Good News is 'The Spirit of the Lord is upon me!' It is that Spirit that has come to release people from bondage to the devil through deliverance ministry. It is that Spirit who endows us with charismatic gifts. The gospel is about power, healing and deliverance. This is also true, but they too are only looking at it from one particular aspect.

Then the evangelical social activists come along and say, 'You are all wrong – Jesus' manifesto is a revamping of Isaiah 61 which is taken, in turn, from Leviticus 25 and it's all to do with the Jubilee! The gospel is all about social and political action'. The Jubilee described in Leviticus was all about tearing up debts, freeing slaves and having a holiday from work. It is quite true that we find all these things in Jesus' manifesto. Even the recovery of sight to the blind has been interpreted as Isaiah's development from slaves in Leviticus to prisoners of war, where they were put in dungeons and could not see. The Hebrew of Isaiah 61 could be interpreted that way, so that to give recovery of sight to the blind is to give back light to those who are in dark dungeons, rather than the healing of the physical eye.

The conservative evangelical is seeing these verses in relation to the soul, or the mind and addressing the mental and soulful faculties of the human being. The charismatic is addressing these verses to the spirit of the person, to the inner being and to the Spirit of God bringing healing and deliverance in a supernatural fashion. The evangelical social activist is applying these words to the body of the individual, their physical situation. What happens is that we fail to recognize that the three parts of the holistic man or woman – spirit, soul and body – are being addressed with the same message, interpreted on three different levels. We must get to the place where we can hold all three aspects together and realise that the gospel is far more full and comprehensive and holistic than our individual theological emphases will lead us to believe. The gospel is for the totality of the human being. It is for his mind, his spirit *and* his body. The three divisions that biblically-minded Christians often fall into really overlap and coalesce into one great holistic gospel for the whole person.

So, how does it look when we see this Kingdom appearing? Already we have read in Luke 4 how the Kingdom proclamation is based on Leviticus 25, revamped into Isaiah 58-61, and then Jesus reads it and says 'today it is fulfilled in your ears'. By the end of this chapter we read 'this is the Good News of the Kingdom'(v43). The Good News of the Kingdom is couched in Jubilee terms, so we are going to look back at Leviticus to see what the Jubilee was all about. This will be important for us as we seek to interpret the Kingdom of God as Jesus proclaims it at the beginning of his ministry.

# 9

# *The King's Jubilee*

I remember some years ago, a union official in this country, saying that we must get away from the Old Testament, religious idea that work is virtuous. That is rather odd because if you read the Old Testament you would find that God does not seem to be too keen on work either. After six days of working on creation he has a rest, and then he incorporates that into the Jewish structure of society in a way that no other society ever has.

The first seven verses of Leviticus 25 speak about the Sabbath. 'Then the Lord spoke to Moses at Mount Sinai, saying, "Speak to the Sons of Israel, and say 'six years you shall sow your field, and six years you shall prune your vineyard and gather in its crop and the seventh year the land shall have a Sabbath rest, a Sabbath to the Lord.'"' It continues about Sabbaths through to verse 7 so that the workers, the male and female slaves, the foreign residents, the aliens, the cattle and the animals and even the crops in the fields all have a rest. No work done for a year.

Once a week, Israel had a complete day of rest; three times a year they would have a three week holiday (a statutory holiday) built into their contract. They had to go up to Jerusalem and so they allowed for a couple of odd days at each end for the travelling, which means it probably worked out to be about a month altogether. That ends up at a month's holiday in twelve, plus the one day off every week. Moreover, believe it or not, after six years, the seventh year was a total Sabbath year (Lev. 23:1-7). That entire seventh year, you did not do any work at all.

Sabbaths were fundamental in Israel's society. After seven rounds of Sabbath years (49 years altogether), the 50th year was the Jubilee. They had just had the previous year off – the 49th year – and then they would hear the trumpet blast which signified that the Jubilee had come round and they had *another* year's holiday! God is really into holidays, and even the Law required that Israel recognized this. The Law stated 'This is a list of the works that you have to do to please God – one, two, three, four…, oh, but incidentally, this one says "do not work!"' It was pointing forward to the day when we shall cease from our own works and enter into rest. He that has ceased from his own works has entered into rest (Heb. 4:10). How are you going to get to heaven? 'Well, I have ceased from my own works and I am having a Sabbath!' How are you going to live out the Christian life? 'I have ceased from my own works and I am letting Jesus live in me!' How are you going to live so that people glorify the Father instead of you? 'Well it is Christ living in me, so I just need to rest in him!' (Mt. 11:28-30).

Thus even the Law, which was perverted by Judaism into a means of attaining holiness and heaven by our own works, even the Old Testament had Sabbath rest built into the very heart of it: 'Cease from your works, because it is only God's work that is going to formulate a relationship.' This was written in, very clearly, right the way through the Old Testament. The Pharisees had got it totally, completely and utterly wrong – and I don't just mean the first century ones, but also Christian Pharisees today. Even the Old Testament, which revolves around the Law, was teaching us grace. The teaching about good works, was teaching us that we can't do them, they have got to be done by God's love in us, as we Sabbath from our own works.

However, in spite of God's grace in the matter, the Jubilee was not fulfilled by Israel, and neither were the Sabbaths. It was for this reason that the children of Israel were put into exile. In fact, Jeremiah explained that the Exile would last for 70 years in order that the land might fulfil its rest. That would account for every seventh Sabbath year plus the odd Jubilee thrown in every 50 years over a period of 490 years. For 490 years, the people of Israel did not keep the Sabbath or the Jubilee. In either the 15th or 13th century BC they entered into the Promised Land, and then right the way through to 606 BC when Nebuchadnezzar came into power and the Exile took place (in 586 BC), you have roughly a 500 or 600 year period. It is most of that period (490 years give or take) that is being compensated for by the 70 years. That was what the judgement of the Exile was all about – that the land might enjoy its Sabbaths.

The Jubilee legislation is found in Leviticus 25:8 'You are also to count off seven Sabbaths of years for yourself. Seven times seven years, so that you have the time of seven Sabbaths of years, namely forty-nine years. You shall then consecrate the fiftieth year[7] and proclaim a release'. Now the fiftieth year was almost certainly the first year of the next seven. So the next seven years would have a Sabbath year number one and Sabbath year number seven:

> You shall thus consecrate the fiftieth year and proclaim a release through the land to all its inhabitants. It shall be a jubilee for you, and each of you shall return to his own property, and each of you shall return to his family. You shall have the fiftieth year as a jubilee; you shall not sow, nor reap its aftergrowth, nor gather in from its untrimmed vines. For it is a jubilee; it shall be holy to you. You shall eat its crops out of the field.
>
> On this year of jubilee each of you shall return to his own property. If you make a sale, moreover, to your friend or buy from your friend's hand, you shall not wrong one another. Corresponding to the number of years after the jubilee, you shall buy from your friend; he is to sell to you according to the number of years of crops. In proportion to the extent of the years you shall increase its price, and in proportion to the fewness of the years you shall diminish its price, for it is a number of crops he is selling to you. So you shall not wrong one another, but you shall fear your God; for I am the Lord your God (Lev. 25:10-17).

Now the fiftieth year Jubilee began on the tenth day of the seventh month: 'You shall then sound a ram's horn abroad on the tenth day of the seventh month; on the Day of Atonement shall you sound a horn all through your land' (Lev. 25:9). The tenth day of the seventh month was the Day of Atonement and was in itself a Sabbath – you did not work. So the people would sit down on the ground around the Tabernacle, as they did every year, and they would wait for the high priest to make atonement for them. He had to do something for them that they could not do for themselves, that is why it was a Sabbath. They might just as well sit down and rest because they could not make atonement for themselves – just as we have to sit down and watch what Jesus has done for us, because we cannot do it for ourselves. That is the meaning behind the Sabbath, and that is what it means for us to be saved by grace.

On the Day of Atonement, the first day of the Jubilee year, the high priest would take two goats, and one of them, chosen by the dice, was called the 'Lord's goat' and the other was called the 'scapegoat' or the 'azazel'. The scapegoat was to have all the sins of the people confessed over it, and then it was sent off into the wilderness, out of sight. 'Azazel' is a very difficult word (Lev. 16:10). 'But the goat on which the lot for the scapegoat (azazel) fell, shall be presented alive before the Lord, to make atonement upon it and to send it into the wilderness as the scapegoat.' Some theologians have suggested that azazel was the name of a demonic figure, but since the Israelites were commanded not to worship demons (Lev. 17:7) that is very unlikely. The word could also come from a root word meaning 'complete destruction', but the more obvious root word means 'rocky precipice'. These last two ideas give us a better picture of the meaning of the ritual. The scapegoat was to wander around until it fell over a precipice and was completely destroyed – it was intended never to come back into the camp. Having confessed your darkest sins over it, you did not want to be reminded of them again by seeing that little old goat poking its head around your tent door a few days later! It was pushed off into the wilderness never to be seen again, permanently ridding you of the sins of the past year, carrying away your guilt forever.

Meanwhile, the blood of the other goat was carried into the Holy Place and sprinkled before the Mercy Seat. That could only be done by the high priest covered with the clouds of incense. If he entered without the clouds of incense, the Law warned that he would surely die. Upon entering the Holy Place, the Shekinah cloud of glory and light, would descend and mingle with the clouds around the high priest. God and man would mingle, the high priest in the midst, bringing God and his people together – just like the picture of Jesus, the Son of Man, coming as both God and man in the clouds and bringing the two together. There is no mediator between God and ourselves, save the man Christ Jesus.

In the Holy Place, with the sprinkling of the blood around the Mercy Seat, God accepted the offering and there was atonement between God and his people brought about by the God-man, the high priest as the mediator. God and man were brought together as one, and sin, the great divider, was disempowered by the blood. That happened every year to teach the people of Israel the way of salvation, and all they had to do was sit and watch it. It was by grace. It was by Sabbath.

Let us sum up four things that took place on the first day of the Jubilee year, namely the Day of Atonement:

1) **Rest** – The Day of Atonement was a Sabbath day, a day of rest. The people did nothing. That is grace. 'For it is not

by works of righteousness that we have done, but according to His Mercy that He saves us. He that ceased from His own works has entered into rest' (Heb. 4:10). It is not the works of the Law that justify people, but by faith we are saved and we are put right with God. Faith is not a work – it precludes all works (Rom. 4:5). In a sense, you could say that what happened on the Day of Atonement is summed up in Paul's epistle to the Romans:

'...for the demonstration, I say, of His righteousness at the present time, so that He would be just and the justifier of the one who has faith in Jesus*.

Where then is boasting? It is excluded. By what kind of law? Of works? No, but by a law of faith. For we maintain that a man is justified by faith apart from works of the Law. Or is God the God of Jews only? Is He not the God of Gentiles also? Yes, of Gentiles also, since indeed God who will justify the circumcised by faith and the uncircumcised through faith is one.

Do we then nullify the Law through faith? May it never be! On the contrary, we establish the Law.'

(Rom. 3:26–31)

*(Literally, 'the **faithfulness** of Jesus')

It is by faith, not by works. It is by rest (grace), and not by our own efforts and our own earnings that we are put right with God. That is nothing new, in one sense, but it was simply taught to the people of Israel, reiterated to them year by year, established in their Law and traditions that salvation was through faith.

2) **Removal** – When the scapegoat went off into the wilderness, the second important factor came into play. As the sins confessed over the scapegoat were carried away and ultimately destroyed along with it, God was demonstrating the complete removal of sin from his people so that there remained no divide between them. God disposed of everything that stood between him and his people. The Lord was saying 'You owe me nothing, your debts, your sins have been removed from you and carried away'. So too, Romans 4:1-25 reveals how our debts reckoned against us have been removed.

3) **Redemption** – When the people of Israel were put back 'at one' with God, God became their inheritance, as David said in Psalm 16:5. 'Atonement' is simply 'at-one-ment', being 'at one' or reconciled with God. The Levites were not allowed to claim even a little plot of ground, because *God* himself was their inheritance. But likewise, God was the true inheritance of the whole of Israel. They each had their portions of ground, but their true inheritance, relationship with the Lord, was lost through sin. But on the Day of Atonement, God was re-inherited, and that meant that all of God was at their disposal again for them to live on day by day. On that day, the whole of Israel was brought back into a relationship with God, whereby they could live on God and God could live in them and they could share life together, and God would once again walk in the camp and be among his people. Romans 5 and 6 shows us how our inheritance is no longer Adam, but Christ.

4) **Release** – On the Day of Atonement, the people of
Israel knew that the sins that had bound them, Satan
who had tied them down, and their own bondage to self
– always our greatest enemy – had been utterly dealt
with. It was a day of release and liberty. They were free
to come to God and free to live for him. The problem
for many of us is that we are so bound up that we cannot live for God. We want to live for him, but we need
to be delivered. The Day of Atonement meant deliverance so that they were free people again. As the Israelites
were no longer in bondage to Pharoah at the Exodus, so
we are freed from sin, Satan and self in Christ. God had
broken those bonds through the high priest sprinkling
the blood of the goat and through the banishment of the
scapegoat. These are pictures of the work of Christ and
we can read about this in Romans 7 and 8.

These four things, rest, removal, redemption and release, all
occur in Romans. **Romans 3**: Sabbath rest, faith not works.
**Romans 4**: Removal of our transgressions, so we owe God
nothing. **Romans 5-6**: we are reconciled to Christ so that
we have an inheritance in him, whereby we can now live
the Christian life. **Romans 7-8**: we are released from sin
and self and the law, and enter into the liberty of the sons of
God.

Atonement constitutes a vertical 'putting-right' between
us and the transcendent God. We worship and enjoy God
because he is other than us and we can talk to him, face to
face. It is not a case of meditating in the depths of our being
so that God, who ends up being just a bit of you, somehow

lurks up from your subconscious. That is Eastern religion. But the God who is *out there*, who has a face and is a person differentiated from what he has made, is the very same God who is *in here*, in our hearts. That means that our at-one-ment will have a horizontal effect too.

If two Christians are at one with God 'out there', and he is the same God who lives within them, how can they fail to be at one with each other? Our oneness as Christians is not just because we have something in common, like all being members of a big religious club it is a oneness which is absolutely, fundamentally divine. I have been put right with the transcendent God who has become an immanent God, and that immanent God who is found in you is at one with me. Therefore, you must be at one with me otherwise we have problems. Our relationships with each other are fundamentally founded on our relationship with God. It is those relationships that demonstrate whether or not we are at one with God, because if I am not at one with you, it must reflect that I am not at one with God who is in you.

Therefore, if you want to know whether a person is reconciled to God, look at their church relationships to see if they are reconciled to each other. That is thoroughly New Testament. That is why, if you bring a gift for God and have something against your brother, you leave it. You do not go ahead and pretend you are at one with God, you go and get right with your brother and thereby get right with God (Mt. 5:23-24).

By the 19th century or so, people began to have an individualistic attitude to their church-going (no doubt born out of the 18th century Enlightenment). 'I have come here to worship God, not to talk to you!' Now in the 21st century, the trend is 'I don't need to go to church to worship God, I can do that by myself, in my bedroom, up in the mountains, out in the fields...' I used to say that to Christians who invaded my privacy. I never did it, mind you, but it sounded good! To worship the transcendent God you do not need to go to church. But to worship the immanent God, the Immanuel God, with us and in us and close to us, you need to find an 'us'! We go to church to meet God in each other. I can meet him out there, but I can also meet him in you. That is the people of God. The reason for going to church to worship is that we believe in the Pentecostal God who actually lives in us and dwells in our midst, and that we find him there in each other.

The Day of Atonement put the Israelites into a vertical relationship with the transcendent God. The Jubilee year which then ensued was a year for demonstrating that relationship horizontally with the immanent God (who, of course, is one and the same) and his people in whom he can be found.

Knowing the Lord intimately implies that we have to begin to know each other better. That is what the Jubilee is. If I am put right with God and given Sabbath rest and grace, and if I can cease from my own works in my relationship with him, then I should be able to give you rest and grace, and vice versa. Our relationships were not meant to be the warring hostility they are in some churches. Jesus said, 'My yoke is easy, my burden is light'. It is transgressors who have a heavy yoke. 'Come unto Me all you that labour and are heavy laden, I will give you rest (Sabbath). Take my yoke upon you and learn of Me.' We are here to ease people's lives, to bring rest and to pour grace into relationships.

If, like on the Day of Atonement, I have found that my relationship with God is a gift that was given to me without my works to earn it, then our relationships together should reflect that grace. Jesus on the Cross has borne all our sins. If God says to me 'You owe me nothing' then I should say to you, horizontally, 'You owe me nothing'. We are in the business of serving out of total freedom, voluntary love and graciousness. If we demand that people owe us, we will kill off the church one by one. Instead, we aim to forgive one another freely, easily and regularly, and we go out of our way to make sure that our accounts with one another are short.

When the Israelite returned for the Jubilee to his original inheritance, the family farm, he would find many more family members gathering there than when he left, since families tend to multiply when left for fifty years. 'Each of you shall return to his own property and each to his own family' (Lev. 25:10-11). The Jubilee Israelite rediscovered family, and so do we when we realise that we share a common inheritance in Christ, and that we live in it together (Rom. 5:21).

Similarly, Jesus brings us freedom from our oppressors, therefore we must give freedom to one another. When we make use of people and seek to control, manoeuvre and manipulate them so that they serve our interests and purposes, we are denying the freedom wherewith Christ has made us free. Rather, we are here to release people into the glorious liberty of the children of God, to become the people God intended them to be (Rom. 8:21).

When the church starts to look like this, we are living together as Kingdom people in Jubilee grace. No wonder when Jesus preached the Kingdom with its Jubilee roots people got excited! He was talking about **rest** from our labouring to please God, but never quite making it. He was talking about the **removal** of the guilt and sin that clouds our lives and steals our joy. He was talking about **reconciliation** with God, who seemed so far off but in reality has drawn near for me to inherit his resources. He was talking about *release* from bondage to sin, Satan and self, and the things that damage our relationships with each other.

Because God has freed me, I am here to declare you free! As I forgive you and release you and serve you rather than demanding things from you, I free you. We free each other in the body by following Jesus' example and washing each other's feet. That is the expression of the emancipation that should characterise the people of God. When we invite people to be a part of that Kingdom life, we are inviting them to share a common life and a common inheritance with us. We are inviting them into Jubilee!

Our relationship together as Kingdom people not only involves restful Jubilee faith which allows us to be at one with the Father and each other, but also the aggressive faith which will fight the spiritual powers of darkness. There is a resting faith in our relationship with the Father. There is an aggressive faith in relationship to the enemy and the advance of the Kingdom.

To exert and wield the authority of Christ is to exert God's kingship into all the world. In all areas, spirit, soul, body, relationships, society, the Kingdom is to begin to spread a net over the world. Jesus says in Matthew 13:47-50:

> Again the kingdom of heaven is like a dragnet cast into the sea, and gathering fish of every kind; and when it was filled, they drew it up on the beach; and they sat down, and gathered the good fish into containers, but the bad they threw away. So it will be at the end of the age; the angels shall come forth and take out the wicked from among the righteous, and will cast them into the furnace of fire; there shall be weeping and gnashing of teeth.

The kingdom net will gather in all the peoples of the earth once the Good News has been proclaimed in all the world: 'And the gospel of the kingdom shall be preached in the whole world for a witness to all the nations, and then the end shall come' (Mt. 24:14). We could extend Jesus' interpretation, without undermining his meaning, by imagining that each knot in the net is a local church, and the joining rope is the Holy Spirit, exerted in kingdom power out of each church in all directions.

When the world has been covered with churches, then the net will be spread and the Spirit can stream into every corner of the world carrying the kingdom with it. When the good news of the Kingdom is preached in all the world, then the end will come and Jesus will remove from the net all that have not submitted to him. God will be 'kinging it' in every area of life. He will throw out the bad fish and leave the good behind until the totality of the Kingdom will be revealed, with nothing offensive caught in it, and the kingdom of this world will become the Kingdom of our Lord and of his Christ (Rev. 11:15). So, the church is the instrument of God's Kingdom. We are the agents of God's war, fighting to bring in God's programme of reform. Of course, 'our fight is not against flesh and blood, but against rulers and powers, the world forces of this darkness and the spiritual forces of wickedness in the heavenly places' (Eph. 6:12).

By understanding the Kingdom, we understand our mission in the world. Christ uses his body, the church, to effect his Will or rule into the earth. The church enters into the sphere of the Kingdom in order to receive it, or take it and thus use it.

So, the Kingdom of God is to be exerted by the church, in the power of the Holy Spirit, into all of the enemy-occupied domain to bring forth fruit and transform society. When the central message of Jesus is once again the central message of the church, we can anticipate the quick fulfilment of the end, the final aspect of the eschatological intervention of our God in the Second Coming of Christ. The blessings of tears wiped away, the final defeat of death, the experience of healings and deliverances in every situation, together with perfect justice, peace and joy will then be achieved.

Amen. Come, Lord Jesus, come quickly!

# Endnotes

[1] John uses 'Life' as an equivalent to Kingdom, as is true in the synoptic gospels (c.f. Mark 9:43, 45, 47 et alia).

[2] Although John records Jesus using 'Kingdom' only 5 times, he does use the word 'Life' and its derivatives 56 times. Comparing the Synoptics, we find that 'Kingdom' and 'Life' are used as equivalents, c.f. Mark 9:43, 45 & 47.

[3] 'Son of Man' cannot be the First Man, because 'Son' requires a man who went before, a predecessor. He must therefore be at least the Second Man – and hence Pauline terminology.

[4] The word translated 'serve' in verse 14 is used nine times in the Old Testament and every occasion is in Daniel. Each time it refers to a divine being – Dan 3:12, 14, 17, 18 & 28, 6:16 & 20, 7:14 & 27.

[5] c.f. also Matt 25:40

[6] c.f. also Isaiah 49:3-6 and John 15:1 where Jesus is the *true* vine.

[7] There was a controversy as to whether the forty-ninth year itself was the Jubilee, but clearly the simplest solution is that it is the fiftieth year. After the forty-nine years with its seven Sabbaths came the extra Sabbath year, a fiftieth year Jubilee.